INTERNATIONAL CRIMINAL COURT:
OVERVIEW AND SELECTED LEGAL ISSUES

INTERNATIONAL CRIMINAL COURT:
OVERVIEW AND SELECTED LEGAL ISSUES

JENNIFER ELSEA

Novinka Books
New York

Senior Editors: Susan Boriotti and Donna Dennis
Coordinating Editor: Tatiana Shohov
Office Manager: Annette Hellinger
Graphics: Wanda Serrano
Editorial Production: Vladimir Klestov, Matthew Kozlowski, Tom Moceri,
 Anthony T. Sovik and Maya Columbus
Circulation: Ave Maria Gonzalez, Vera Popovic, Luis Aviles, Raymond Davis,
 Melissa Diaz and Jeannie Pappas
Marketing: Cathy DeGregory

Library of Congress Cataloging-in-Publication Data
Available Upon Request

ISBN: 1-59033-557-0.

Copyright © 2003 by Novinka Books, An Imprint of
 Nova Science Publishers, Inc.
 400 Oser Ave, Suite 1600
 Hauppauge, New York 11788-3619
 Tele. 631-231-7269   Fax 631-231-8175
 e-mail: Novascience@earthlink.net
 Web Site: http://www.novapublishers.com

All rights reserved. No part of this book may be reproduced, stored in a retrieval system or transmitted in any form or by any means: electronic, electrostatic, magnetic, tape, mechanical photocopying, recording or otherwise without permission from the publishers.

The authors and publisher have taken care in preparation of this book, but make no expressed or implied warranty of any kind and assume no responsibility for any errors or omissions. No liability is assumed for incidental or consequential damages in connection with or arising out of information contained in this book.

This publication is designed to provide accurate and authoritative information with regard to the subject matter covered herein. It is sold with the clear understanding that the publisher is not engaged in rendering legal or any other professional services. If legal or any other expert assistance is required, the services of a competent person should be sought. FROM A DECLARATION OF PARTICIPANTS JOINTLY ADOPTED BY A COMMITTEE OF THE AMERICAN BAR ASSOCIATION AND A COMMITTEE OF PUBLISHERS.

Printed in the United States of America

CONTENTS

Preface		vii
Chapter 1	Introduction and Negotiating History	1
Chapter 2	Structure of the ICC	9
Chapter 3	Jurisdiction	17
Chapter 4	Rules of Procedure and Evidence	37
Chapter 5	Implications for the United States as Non-Member	51
Chapter 6	Congressional Action	57
Index		63

PREFACE

The International Criminal Court (ICC) is the first global permanent international court with jurisdiction to prosecute individuals for "the most serious crimes of concern to the international community." The United Nations, many human rights organizations, and most democratic nations have expressed support for the new court. The Bush Administration firmly opposes it and has formally renounced the U.S. obligations under the treaty. At the same time, however, the Administration has stressed that the United States shares the goals of the ICC's supporters-promotion of the rule of law-and does not intend to take any action to undermine the ICC.

The primary objection given by the U.S. in opposition to the treaty is the ICC's possible assertion of the jurisdiction over U.S. soldiers charged with "war crimes" resulting from legitimate uses of force. The main issue faced by the current Congress is whether to adopt a policy aimed at preventing the ICC from becoming effective or whether to continue contributing to the development of the ICC in order to improve it.

This book provides a historical background of the negotiations for the Rome Statute, outlines the structure of the International Criminal Court (ICC) as contained in the final Statute, and describes the jurisdiction of the ICC. The book further identifies the specific crimes enumerated in the Rome Statute as supplemented by the draft elements of crime. A discussion of procedural safeguards follows, including reference to the draft procedural rules.

The book then goes on to discuss the implications for the United States as a non-ratifying country when the ICC comes into being, and outlines some legislation enacted and proposed to regulate U.S relations with the ICC.

Chapter 1

INTRODUCTION AND NEGOTIATING HISTORY

On April 11, 2002, the Rome Statute of the International Criminal Court[1] received its sixtieth ratification, meaning it will come into effect July 1, 2002, years earlier than had been predicted. The ICC will be the first global permanent international court with jurisdiction to prosecute individuals for "the most serious crimes of concern to the international community;"[2] the United Nations, many human rights organizations, and most democratic nations have expressed support for the new court.[3] The Bush Administration, however, firmly opposes it and has taken the measure of formally renouncing any U.S. obligations under the treaty.[4] Some critics

---

[1] U.N. Doc. NCONF.183/9 (1988)("Rome Statute").
[2] These include genocide, crimes against humanity, war crimes, and potentially the crime of aggression, if the Assembly of States Parties is able to reach an agreement defining it. Rome Statute art. 5(1). *See infra* text accompanying note 98.
[3] *See* Barbara Crossette, *World Criminal Court is Ratified - Praised by UN., Opposed by U.S.*, N.Y. TIMES Apr. 12, 2002, *available at* 2002 WL-NYT 0210200003. For the current status of signatures, ratifications and reservations, visit http://untreaty.un.orgi ENGLISH/bible/englishinternetbible/partI/chapterXVIII/treaty 10.asp.
[4] *See* Jonathon Wright, *U.S. Renounces Obligations to International Court*, 'REUTERS, May 6, 2002. Although some in the media have described the act as an "unsigning" of the treaty, it may be more accurately described as a notification of intent not to ratify. The letter from Under Secretary of State for Arms Control and International Security John R. Bolton to the U.N. Secretary General stated:

> This is to inform you, in connection with the Rome Statute of the International Criminal Court adopted on July 17, 1998, that the United States does not intend to become a party to the treaty. Accordingly, the United States has no legal obligations arising from its signature on December 31, 2000. The United States requests that its intention not to become a party, as expressed in this letter, be reflected in the depositary's status lists relating to this treaty.

have remarked that the issue is causing a rift between the United States and its allies in the war against terrorism.[5] At the same time, the Administration has stressed that the United States shares the goal of the ICC's supporters - promotion of the rule of law - and does not intend to take any action to undermine the ICC.[6] In a move that may foreshadow the Administration's strategy, the United States is also reportedly seeking assurances from the United Nations that no U.N. personnel taking part in the peacekeeping mission in East Timor will be subject to prosecution by any local or international court for war crimes - a move that has met with resistance from U.S. allies because they say it could undermine the principles of the ICC.[7]

While the United States initially supported the idea of creating an international criminal court[8] and was a major participant at the Rome

---

Reprinted at http://www.state.gov/r/pa/prs/ps/2002/9968.htm.

[5] *See Give it a Welcome - The Coming World Criminal Court*, ECONOMIST (London), Apr. 13, 2002, available at 2002 WL 7245784; James Bone, War Crimes Court Pits United States Against the World, TIMES OF LONDON, Apr. 11, 2002, available at 2002 WL 4198476; Stuart Taylor Jr., Be Wary of the War Crimes Court, but Not Too Wary, NAT'L J., Apr. 6,2002, available at 2002 WL7094917.

[6] *See* Marc Grossman, Under Secretary for Political Mairs, Remarks to the Center for Strategic and International Studies, Washington, D.C., (May 6, 2002) (prepared remarks available at http://www.state.gov/p/9949pf.htm). Secretary Grossman promised that:

> Notwithstanding our disagreements with the Rome Treaty, the United States respects the decision of those nations who have chosen to join the ICC; but they in turn must respect our decision not to join the ICC or place our citizens under the jurisdiction of the court.
> So, despite this difference, we must work together to promote real justice after July 1, when the Rome Statute enters into force.

The existence of a functioning ICC will not cause the United States to retreat from its leadership role in the promotion of international justice and the rule of law.

[7] *See* Colum Lynch, *U.S. Seeb Court Immunity for E. Timor Peacekeepers*, WASH. POST May 16,2002 at A22, *available at* 2002 WL 20709611 (reporting there are currently no U.S. troops serving in U.N. missions); Edith M. Lederer, *U.S. Makes Int'l Court Demands*, AP May 20, 2002, *available at* 2002 WL 21234979 (reporting that France, Britain, Ireland, Norway, and Colombia oppose the U.S. request).

[8] *See* Ruth Wedgwood, Harold K. Jacobson and Monroe Leigh, *The United States and the Statute of Rome*, 95 AM. J. INT'L L. 124 (2001) (commenting that the United States has "repeatedly and publicly declared its support in principle" for an international criminal court). Congress expressed its support for such a court, providing the rights of U.S. citizens were recognized. *See, e.g.,* Foreign Operations Appropriations Act § 599E, P.L. 101-513, 104 Stat. 2066-2067 (1990)(expressing the sense of the Congress that "the United States should explore the need for the establishment of an International Criminal Court" and that "the establishment of such a court or courts for the more effective prosecution of international criminals should not derogate from established standards of due process, the rights of the accused to a fair trial and the sovereignty of individual nations"); Anti-Drug Abuse Act of 1988 § 4108, P.L. 100-690, 102 Stat. 4181, 4266 (1988)(encouraging the President to initiate discussions with foreign governments about the possibility of creating an

Conference,[9] in the end, the United States - joined by Iran, Iraq, China, Israel, Sudan, and Libya - voted against the Statute.[10] Nevertheless, President Clinton signed the treaty December 31, 2000 - the last day it was open for signature without simultaneous ratification, at the same time declaring that the treaty contained "significant flaws" and that he would not submit it to the Senate for its advice and consent "until our fundamental concerns are satisfied."[11] The Bush Administration has likewise declined to submit the Rome Statute to the Senate for ratification, and has notified the depositary of the United Nations of the U.S. intent not to ratify the treaty.[12] The primary objection given by the United States in opposition to the treaty is the ICC's possible assertion of jurisdiction over U.S. soldiers charged with "war crimes" resulting from legitimate uses of force, even if the United States does not ratify the Rome Statute. The United States sought to exempt U.S. soldiers and employees from the jurisdiction of the ICC based on the unique position the United States occupies with regard to international peacekeeping.[13] The main issue faced by the Congress is the level of cooperation to allow between the United States and the ICC: to withhold all cooperation from the ICC and its member nations in order to prevent the ICC from becoming effective, to continue contributing to the development of the ICC in order to improve it, or to adopt a pragmatic approach based solely on U.S. interests.[14]

---

international court to try persons accused of having engaged in international drug trafficking or having committed international crimes, providing constitutional guarantees of U.S. citizens are recognized); P.L. 99-399, Sec. 1201 (1986)

[9] See U.N. International Criminal Court: Hearings before the Subcomm. on International Operations of the Senate Foreign Relations Committee 105tb Congo (1998) (testimony of David J. Scheffer, Ambassador-at-Large for War Crimes Issues).

[10] See Wedgwood, *et al., supra* note 8, at 124 (noting that the final vote for the Statute was 120 in favor to seven against).

[11] Statement on the Rome Treaty on the International Criminal Court, Dec. 31, 2000, 37(1) Weekly Compilation of Presidential Documents 4 (2001).

[12] Because the United States signed the Rome Statute, it had been obligated under international law to refrain from conducting activity in contravention of the object and purpose of the treaty. *See* Vienna Convention on the Law of Treaties, *opened for signature* May 23,1969, art. 18, 1155 U.N.T.S. 335. However, this obligation ends once a signatory state has indicated an intent *not* to ratify the treaty. *Id.* Some press reports initially indicated the Administration was also planning to renounce the Vienna Convention. *See* Neil A. Lewis, *U.S. to 'Unsign' Treaty, Disavow World Tribunal,* SAN DIEGO UNION & TRIB., May 5,2002 at Al. The report was apparently based on a misunderstanding of the Administration's statement explaining the intent behind its action, which was reportedly to avoid any obligations on the part of the United States that may have been incurred through its signature of the Rome Statute, in accordance with article 18 of the Vienna Convention.

[13] *See* Grossman, *supra* note 6.

[14] *See* David J. Scheffer, *Staying the Course with the International Criminal Court,* 35 CORNELL INT'L L.J. 47 (2000) (arguing the United States could most effectively influence the shape of the ICC through cooperating with it rather than impeding it).

This report provides an historical background of the negotiations for the Rome Statute, outlines the structure of the ICC as contained in the final Statute, and describes the jurisdiction of the ICC. The report identifies the specific crimes enumerated in the Rome Statute as supplemented by the draft elements of crime drawn up by the Preparatory Commission established by the Rome Conference. A discussion of procedural safeguards follows, including reference to the draft procedural rules. The report then discusses the implications for the United States, as a non-ratifying country as the ICC comes into being, and outlines some legislation enacted and proposed to regulate U.S. relations with the ICC.

The creation of the ICC is the culmination of a decades-long effort to establish an international court with the jurisdiction to try individuals for the commission of crimes against humanity.[15] The post-World War II tribunals to try Nazi and Japanese war criminals established precedent for the ICC. The later International Criminal Tribunal for Yugoslavia (ICTY) and the International Criminal Tribunal for Rwanda (ICTR) built upon the Nuremberg legacy. However, all of these courts were created *ad hoc* with limited jurisdiction. An international court with jurisdiction over all crimes of the worst nature affecting mankind was urged in order to end impunity for *any and all* perpetrators of large-scale atrocities. The U.N. General Assembly voted to establish an Ad Hoc Committee on the Establishment of an International Criminal Court[16] and created a Preparatory Committee charged with "preparing a widely acceptable consolidated text of a convention for an International Criminal Court as a next step towards consideration by a conference of plenipotentiaries."[17]

The Preparatory Committee held six sessions between March 1996 and April 1998 to prepare a text for consideration at the Rome Conference.[18] The most contentious issue at the Conference revolved around the level of independence the ICC would have vis-a-vis national courts and the U.N. Security Council. The Preparatory Commission considered two basic options for defining the jurisdiction of the ICC: The ICC might assert jurisdiction over all relevant crimes, exercising primacy over national courts, without regard to the nationality of the victims or perpetrators. Under this option,

---

[15] For a general background and discussion of the ICC, see The Rome Statute of the International Criminal Court: Selected Legal and Constitutional Issues, CRS Report RL30091, Feb. 22, 1999; The International Criminal Court Treaty: Description, Policy Issues, and Congressional Concerns, CRS Report RL30020, Jan. 5, 1999.
[16] GA Res. 49/53, U.N. GAOR, 49th Sess., U.N. Doc. NRES/49/53 (1994).
[17] GA Res. 50/46, U.N. GAOR, 50th Sess., U.N. Doc. A/RES/50/46 (1995).
[18] *See* United Nations, "The Draft Statute of the International Criminal Court: Background Information," *available at* http://www.un.org/icc/statute.htm.

"rogue" regimes would be unable to insulate themselves from responsibility for crimes committed against opposing forces or ethnic minorities, even during internal armed conflicts. Many countries, including the United States, objected to the idea as an intrusion into the sovereignty of nations. Second, the ICC's power to try cases could be "complementary" to that of national courts, where the ICC would exercise jurisdiction only when national courts of the country in which the crime took place, or whose national was accused, were unable or unwilling to prosecute. The second model, which the United States had supported, was adopted in principle.[19]

The adoption of the complementarity model of jurisdiction led to the even more intractable question of how and when the ICC would take a case. Possible options included a recommendation by the U.N. Security Council, a recommendation by a country with personal or subject matter jurisdiction over the crime or the accused, or upon the initiative of the ICC itself. Taking the position that treaty regimes should apply only to those states that choose to become parties and not to those that choose to remain outside, the United States delegation offered amendments at Rome to require the consent of both the State in which the crime was allegedly committed and of the state of nationality of the alleged perpetrator, or, failing that, at least of the state of nationality, to the jurisdiction of the Court.[20] Under the U.S. proposals, the ICC would have jurisdiction over citizens of non-consenting non-parties only in cases referred or authorized by the U.N. Security Council, which would have allowed the United States and other permanent members of the Council to veto any attempt to prosecute their citizens, but would allow for the prosecution of state architects of genocidal policies, for example, as long as the political support could be generated in the Security Council.

The conferees rejected this proposal on the grounds that it would essentially mirror the present application of *ad hoc* tribunals, bringing some perpetrators of crimes against humanity to justice while allowing others to escape with impunity.[21] Additionally, in their view, a treaty that subjects citizens of non-parties to an international court's jurisdiction does not bind the non-party state to *do* anything and thus does not infringe on its

---

[19] Rome Statute arts. 12-14.
[20] *See* Johan D. van der Vyver, *Personal and Territorial Jurisdiction of the International Criminal Court*, 14 EMORY INT'L L. REV. 1, 32 (2000).
[21] *See* Wedgwood, *et ai, supra* note 8, at 126 (commenting that the U.S. proposal would "exempt not only U.S. nationals, but also the nationals of rogue states, which are most likely to produce or to harbor war criminals in the future and which are the least likely to consent to having their nationals tried by the ICC").

sovereignty.[22] Aliens who commit crimes are subject to the jurisdiction of local courts in any event. Under this view, assuming that the referring state would have the jurisdiction to try or extradite an alien accused of a crime on its territory, the referring state could just as legitimately cede its jurisdiction over the accused to an international court.[23]

The U.S. delegation also proposed to exempt from the Court's jurisdiction conduct that arises from the official actions of a non-party state acknowledged as such by the non-party. The United States, it was argued, would willingly acknowledge the official nature of conduct related to peacekeeping missions or other foreign affairs activity and thus gain an exemption from the Court's jurisdiction for alleged crimes arising from such missions.[24] This, it proposed, would eliminate the disincentive for non-party States to participate in peacekeeping missions. Dictators, it said, would be reluctant to admit responsibility for conduct that could be viewed as criminal under the Rome Statute. The conference voted to take no action on the proposal.[25] The final rule allows the ICC to take a case on the recommendation of one of the countries with the appropriate jurisdiction, the U.N. Security Council, or the ICC Prosecutor.

The U.S. delegation to Rome, led by David Scheffer, then Ambassador-at-Large for War Crimes Issues, argued that allowing the Prosecutor-to initiate cases would potentially put U.S. military personnel in jeopardy of being summoned in front of the ICC on groundless charges. The United States is in a unique position in the world, Scheffer argued, in which it is frequently called upon to respond to international crises, often by deploying U.S. troops and government officials to hostile countries. If those countries could retaliate by accusing the United States and its officials or military personnel of war crimes, for example, the United States could find itself hamstrung in its peacekeeping efforts. The Rome delegates adopted four methods to accommodate U.S. concerns regarding abuse of prosecutorial discretion: limiting the power of the ICC Prosecutor, requiring the consent of

---

[22] *See id.* at 127 (arguing that "while a non-party state is not itself bound to accept an assertion of jurisdiction over itself unless it has consented, the same is not true of its nationals if they commit offenses in the territory of a state that is a party").

[23] This was the operational theory providing jurisdiction at the Nuremberg tribunals. *See* M. Cherif Bassiouni, *Universal Jurisdiction for International Crimes: Historical Perspectives and Contemporary Practice*, 42 VA. J. INT'L L. 81, 91-92 (2001)(positing that sovereignty does not limit the exercise of criminal jurisdiction to single states)(citing IMT Judgment, Sept. 30, 1946, that signatory states to the London Charter "have done together what anyone of them might have done singly; for it is not to be doubted that any nation has the right thus to set up special courts to administer law.").

[24] *See* van der Vyver, *supra* note 20, at 18 (describing U.S. position with regard to acceptable regimes as an attempt to secure immunity for U.S. citizens).

a country which would have jurisdiction over an alleged crime before initiating a prosecution, narrowly defining the crimes for which a person may be prosecuted, and creating a role for the U.N. Security Council,[26] though not adopting the U.S. suggestion which would have allowed any permanent member of the Security Council to veto any proposed prosecution.

Instead, the Rome Conference adopted the so-called Singapore Proposal, which, rather than requiring unanimity of the permanent members of the Security Council to initiate a prosecution, would require unanimity in order to block prosecution temporarily.[27] Because the Permanent Five would have to cooperate in order to authorize a peace-keeping mission in the first place, it was reasoned, all five could be expected to agree to block any unwarranted ICC prosecutions that might arise.[28] This proposal would not guarantee immunity in the case of a unilateral action on the part of the United States, however, and failed to gain the support of the U.S. delegation.

Although the United States voted against the Rome Statute to establish an ICC, it did sign the Final Act of the Conference.[29] As a consequence, it was able to participate as a voting member of the Preparatory Commission created by the Rome conference. The Preparatory Commission has developed draft rules of procedure and evidence, the elements of crimes, a relationship agreement between the ICC and the U.N., financial regulations, an agreement on privileges and immunities, a budget, and the rules of

---

[25] *See id.*
[26] Rome Statute art. 16 (allowing the Security Council to delay any investigation or prosecution indefinitely). The Security Council can also initiate prosecution under Article 13(b).
[27] *See* Lawrence Weschler, *The United States and the ICC, in* THE UNITED STATES AND THE INTERNATIONAL CRIMINAL CoURT 85, 93 (Sarah B. Sewall and Carl Kaysen, eds. 2000) [hereinafter "THE U.S. AND THE ICC].
[28] *See id.*
[29] U.N. Doc. A/CONF.183/10. The Final Act is separate from the Rome Statute and consists largely of a recitation of the events that led to the convening of the Conference and of the proceedings and decisions at the Conference.

procedure to govern the Assembly of States Parties.[30] It has not yet completed its work on the definition of the crime of aggression.

---

[30] These documents may be found at http://www.un.orgilaw/icc.

Chapter 2

STRUCTURE OF THE ICC

The Rome Statute establishes the Court's structure and provides rules for its limited governance by the states parties to the Statute. The ICC will consist of the Presidency, three Trial Divisions, the Office of the Prosecutor, and the Registry.[31] It will have international legal personality to carry out its functions,[32] and its relationship to the United Nations will be established by agreement between the ICC president and the U.N.[33]

The Rome Statute is designed to provide for the independence of the prosecutor and judges. However, it also provides a system of checks and balances designed to rein in overzealous prosecutors and prevent the ICC from falling under the control of biased judges or states with an interest in the outcome. For example, for a prosecutor to initiate a case, he must first get independent authorization from the ICC's Pre-Trial Chamber to continue an investigation.[34] The statute's requirements for election of judges are designed to diminish the possibility that the pre-trial chamber would be politicized, thereby increasing its ability to prevent prosecutors from bringing unwarranted charges. The candidates for judge are required to be competent in either criminal law or in relevant areas of international law,[35]

---

[31] Rome Statute art. 34.
[32] *Id. art. 4.*
[33] *Id.* art. 2. The Preparatory Commission adopted a draft proposed agreement in the fall of 2000, which will require further action by the Assembly of States Parties once the treaty enters into force in July 2002, in order to become finalized. *See* Draft Relationship Agreement between the United Nations and the International Criminal Court, U.N. Doc. PCNICC/2000/WGICC-UN/L.1 (2000), *available at* http://www.un.org/law/icc/prepcomm/nov2000/english/ wgicclle.pdf.
[34] Rome Statute art. 15.
[35] *Id.* art. 36(3)(b)(i)-(ii).

and no two judges are permitted to be from the same state.[36] The person being investigated may request the disqualification of any judge when the judge's "impartiality might reasonably be doubted."[37] The trial and appellate chambers are kept separate to enable parties to challenge both interlocutory and final decisions before different judges. Finally, it provides mechanisms for checks by majority vote of the Assembly of States Parties, a representative body of the member states.

THE JUDGES OF THE ICC: THE PRESIDENCY AND TRIAL DIVISIONS

A total of eighteen judges will be elected to serve staggered nine-year terms on the ICC, subject to a possible increase in the number of judges upon recommendation by the President and its approval by the Assembly of States Parties. States parties to the ICC may nominate one qualified candidate for each election. Judicial candidates must be nationals of states parties to the Rome Statute, although not necessarily of the nominating state.[38] The Assembly of States Parties may establish an advisory committee on nominations as it deems appropriate.[39] Judges will be selected by vote of the Assembly of States Parties to be representative of the world's population in terms of legal systems, geography, legal specialties, and gender.[40] Judges will not be permitted to pursue outside occupations, and may be removed from office by a vote of two-thirds majority of the Assembly of States Parties to affirm a recommendation by two-thirds of the other judges that the judge be removed for serious misconduct or inability to carry out the functions of the position.[41]

The Presidency consists of a President and two Vice-Presidents, who are to be elected from the judge corps by an absolute majority of its members.[42] The President and Vice Presidents serve for three-year terms, unless their terms as judges expire earlier, with one opportunity for re-election. The President will have overall responsibility for the administration of the Court

---

[36] *Id.* art. 36(7).
[37] See Matthew A Barrett, Note, Ratify or Reject: Examining the United States' Opposition to the International Criminal Court, 28 GA. J. INT'L & COMP. L. 83, 97 (1999) (citing the Rome Statute, art. 41(2)(a)-(b)).
[38] Rome Statute art. 36.
[39] *Id.* art. 36(5).
[40] *Id.* art. 36(8).
[41] *Id.* art. 46.
[42] *Id.* art. 38.

(with the exception of the Office of the Prosecutor) and for other functions, such as deciding which judges will hear which cases and whether to excuse a particular judge or prosecutor from any particular case for reasons of possible conflict of interest.

The 18 judges will be divided among the Pre-Trial Division, Trial Division, and Appeals Division. Judges assigned to the Appeals Division remain there throughout their tenure, while judges initially assigned to the Trial or Pre-Trial Divisions serve three-year terms plus any time necessary to complete ongoing hearings. Judges assigned to the Trial or Pre-Trial Divisions may be temporarily shifted between the two divisions to accommodate the workload of the ICC, but judges assigned to the Appeals Division, which will include the President, may not be temporarily assigned to another division.[43]

The Pre-Trial Division, by majority vote of a three-judge chamber, decides issues regarding admissibility of evidence and jurisdiction of the Court to hear a case, authorizes the prosecutor to pursue self-initiated investigations, determines whether sufficient evidence exists to support an indictment, and issues rulings regarding the withholding of material held by a state that deems the disclosure of such information to be prejudicial to the national security of that state.[44] Other issues may be decided by individual judges, including rulings necessary to ensure privacy and security of witnesses and actions to seek the cooperation of a state in executing one of the majority-issued orders.

The Trial Division consists of two chambers of three judges each and is responsible for the fair and expeditious conduct of trials with proper regard for the rights of the accused and security of witnesses. The Trial Chambers have the authority to decide intermediary issues by majority decision or to refer such issues to the Pre-Trial Division. They are responsible for confirming that the accused understands the nature of the charges and that pleas are voluntary, and for providing an accurate transcript of 'the proceedings.' The Trial Division also sentences the accused upon conviction, based on all relevant evidence supplemented by means of additional hearings, when necessary.[45]

The Appeals Division consists of a single chamber of five judges, including the ICC President, that hears appeals of convictions, sentences, and acquittals, as well as interlocutory rulings on admissibility of evidence, jurisdiction, and the like. The Appeals Chamber has powers comparable to

---

[43] *Id.* art. 39.
[44] *Id.* art. 57.
[45] *Id.* art. 76.

those of the Trial Division, and may reverse or amend a decision or sentence, or it may order a new trial before a different chamber.[46] A convicted person or his survivors or designee may bring an appeal any time new evidence becomes available that could have changed the outcome of a case.

The Appeals Division may reject such an application it determines to be unfounded, or it may order new proceedings before the original or a new Trial Chamber, or retain jurisdiction over the matter.[47] In cases of grave and manifest miscarriages of justice, it may award compensation to an arrested or convicted person.[48]

PROSECUTOR

The Prosecutor is selected by an absolute majority of the Assembly of States Parties via secret ballot.[49] The Assembly then votes, again in secret, to select Deputy Prosecutors from a list of candidates provided by the Prosecutor. The Prosecutor and Deputy Prosecutors are each eligible to hold office for one nine-year term, without the possibility of re-election. During their terms in office, they may not engage in any activities that might place their impartiality in doubt, and any of them may be disqualified from a particular case by the Appeals Chamber if the person being investigated or prosecuted so requests. If it is found that the Prosecutor has committed serious misconduct, breached his or her duties, or is no longer able to carry out his or her functions under the Statute, an absolute majority of the Assembly may decide by secret ballot to disqualify him or her. A Deputy Prosecutor may be removed for like reasons by an absolute majority of the Assembly upon the recommendation of the Prosecutor. In either proceeding, the Prosecutor or Deputy Prosecutor is allowed to present and receive evidence in order to dispute the charges.

The Office of the Prosecutor receives referrals from the U.N. Security Council and member states on possible crimes within the jurisdiction of the Court for investigation to determine whether prosecution is warranted. The Rome Statute also allows investigations to be initiated by the Prosecutor, subject to approval by the majority of a Pre-Trial Chamber. The Prosecutor determines whether the information available establishes a reasonable basis

---

[46] *Id.* art. 83.
[47] *Id.* art. 84.
[48] *Id.* art. 85.
[49] *Id.* art. 42.

to conduct an investigation.[50] If there is such a basis, the Prosecutor shall "extend the investigation to cover all facts and evidence relevant to an assessment of whether there is criminal responsibility under [the Rome] Statute," giving equal consideration to exonerating evidence as is given to incriminating information, and taking care to respect the interests of victims and witnesses, as well as the rights of the accused.[51] The Prosecutor may conduct investigations on the territory of a state that is a party to the Statute or agrees to cooperate.[52]

The role of the ICC Prosecutor remains a point of contention for the United States, which sought more limits on the power of the Prosecutor to launch cases on his own initiative. The U.S. opposed granting this discretion to the Prosecutor on the grounds it would "encourage overwhelming the Court with complaints and risk diversion of its resources, as well as embroil the Court in controversy, political decision making, and confusion."[53]

REGISTRY

The Office of the Registry is responsible under the Rome Statute for the non-judicial administration of the Court,[54] including providing for witness protection and assistance, as well as for receiving prisoners, arranging for the defense of indigents, and surrendering convicted persons to the state of incarceration. The Registrar, who will head the Registry as the chief administrative officer of the Court, is elected by an absolute majority of the judges by secret ballot after considering the Assembly's recommendations. The Registrar serves on a full-time basis for up to two five-year terms. Deputy registrars may serve shorter terms and need not serve full-time.

As part of its duties with regard to witnesses, the Registrar is responsible for the creation of the Victims and Witnesses Unit (VWU), which will be charged with recommending and providing protection, counseling, and assistance to witnesses and victims who appear before the Court, as well as others who may be placed at risk due to testimony given by other witnesses,

---

[50] *Id.* art. 53.
[51] *Id.* art. 54.
[52] *Id.* arts. 54 and 87(5).
[53] Developments at the Rome Treaty Conference: Hearings before the Senate Comm. on Foreign Relations, 105th Cong. (1998) (statement of David Scheffer, Ambassador-at-Large for War Crimes Issues). For more detail about the procedure for Prosecutor-initiated investigations, see *infra* text accompanying notes 125 *et seq.*
[54] Rome Statute art. 43.

in order to prevent their suffering mental or physical violence.[55] VWU staff must have expertise in treating trauma victims, including children and victims of sex crimes and violence.

The Rome Statute does not provide for a separate unit within the Registry to provide its mandated support to the defense.[56] However, draft Rules of Procedure and Evidence, Rule 20[57] requires the Registrar to organize the staff of the Registry "in a manner that promotes the rights of the defense, consistent with the principle of fair trial," and to perform certain duties in order to ensure the independence of defense counsel, providing the defense with support, facilities, and information; helping the accused to obtain the assistance of competent legal counsel;[58] and cooperating with state defense and bar associations. The Registrar is responsible for drafting a list of criteria for assigning defense counsel[59] and a code of professional responsibility for all counsel.[60]

ASSEMBLY OF STATES PARTIES

The Assembly of States Parties is not an organ of the ICC, but is comprised of a representative of each ratifying state, with each state having one vote.[61] Non-party states who have signed the Rome Statute or its Final Act may participate as observers but may not vote. The Assembly provides management and oversight to the Presidency, the Prosecutor, and the Registrar regarding the administration of the ICC, including the budget, the number of judges, and rules of procedure and evidence. The Assembly also makes determinations in the event a state party fails to comply with a request to cooperate, or refers the matter to the U.N. Security Council if the case was referred to the ICC by that body. The Assembly also elects 21 persons to

---

[55] *Id.* art. 43(6).
[56] *See* Christopher Keith Hall, *The First Five Sessions of the U.N. Preparatory Commission for the International Criminal Court*, 94 AM. J. INT'L L. 773, 783 (2000)(describing initiative on the part of Canada, France, Germany, and the Netherlands to address the issue).
[57] Draft Rule of Procedure and Evidence (RPE) Report of the Preparatory Commission for the International Criminal Court; Addendum: Finalized Draft Text of the Rules of Procedure and Evidence, U.N. Doc. PCNICC/2000/INF/3/Add.1 (2000), *available at* http:// www.iccnow.org/html/un.html [hereinafter Draft RPE].
[58] Draft RPE 22 requires that counsel have "established competence in international or criminal law and procedure, as well as the necessary relevant experience, whether as judge, prosecutor, advocate or in other similar capacity, in criminal proceedings."
[59] *See* Draft RPE 21.
[60] *See* Draft RPE 8.
[61] *See* Rome Statute art. 112. The right to vote may be suspended if a state party falls in arrears of its payments for more than two full years. *Id.* art. 112(8).

serve three-year terms as members of the Bureau, and it may establish other subsidiary bodies to carry out oversight functions.

The Assembly of States Parties may amend the Rome Statute in accordance with art. 121. After seven years have passed since the Statute has entered into force, any state party may propose an amendment, which will be adopted if a two-thirds majority of the Assembly of States Parties votes in its favor. Amendments enter into force for all states parties one year after seven-eighths of the states parties have deposited their instruments of ratification or acceptance with the U.N. Secretary-General. Any state party which has not accepted the amendment may withdraw from the Statute with immediate effect by giving notice within one year after its entry into force.

Critics of the Rome Statute question the future ability of the Assembly of States Parties to exercise any real accountability over the operations of the ICC.[62] They predict that the one-vote-per-state rule could lend lopsided sway to tiny countries,[63] and complain that the Statute does not provide for the democratic accountability of a state's representative at the Assembly to the citizens of the state. Critics also note that representatives will be able to vote at the Assembly and influence the development of the ICC even though they may represent non-democratic countries with poor human rights records or who are proclaimed adversaries of the United States.[64]

---

[62] See Lee A. Casey, *The Case Against the International Criminal Court*, 25 FORDHAM INT'L L.J. 840, 845-46(2002) (arguing that the Assembly of States Parties will be a "congress of ambassadors from different and hostile interests" that can claim "no democratic legitimacy even on a theory of virtual representation").

[63] See id. at 844.

[64] See id. at 845.

Chapter 3

JURISDICTION

SUBJECT MATTER JURISDICTION

Article 5 of the final Statute limits the jurisdiction of the ICC to the "most serious crimes of concern to the international community as a whole," namely, genocide, crimes against humanity, war crimes and, potentially, aggression and terrorism.[65] Article 8 of the final Statute limits the ICC's jurisdiction over "war crimes" primarily to those committed as "part of a plan or policy or as part of a large-scale commission of such crimes."[66]

The ICC's jurisdiction will extend only to crimes committed after its inception. However, the Statute allows states parties to the Statute to opt out of the ICC's jurisdiction over war crimes for a period of seven years after becoming a party, as well as its jurisdiction over any new crimes that may be added to the Statute in the future.[67] The United States had wanted an initial opt-out provision that would have allowed states parties to assess the effectiveness and impartiality of the Court for a longer period of time with respect to all of the covered crimes before deciding whether to submit to the full jurisdiction of the Court. However, the proposal was rejected, as was a U.S. proposal allowing non-states parties to opt out (or in) for the ICC's jurisdiction over specific crimes. Thus, the ICC appears initially to have broader jurisdiction over war crimes allegedly committed by citizens of non-

---

[65] Rome Statute art. 5. The preparatory committee was unable to reach a consensus on a definition for the crime of "aggression."
[66] *Id.* art. 8.
[67] *Id.* arts. 124 and 121.

member states than it will have over war crimes allegedly committed by citizens of states that ratify the treaty.[68]

The elements of each of the crimes, drafted largely at the insistence of the U.S. negotiating team,[69] will likely be adopted once the ICC comes into existence and should serve to check the discretion of the ICC judges and prosecutor.[70] The draft elements may also help to resolve any possible problems caused by vagueness, inherent in international treaties due to the perceived elevated importance of compromise over clarity, but seen as detrimental to fairness in enforcing criminal law, which requires specificity.[71] The Rome Statute provides for amendment of the elements of crimes by two-thirds vote of the Assembly of State Parties. The crimes and their draft elements are summarized below.

Genocide

The Preparatory Committee borrowed the language regarding the crime of genocide used in the 1948 Genocide Convention,[72] which prohibits a number of acts when carried out "with intent to destroy, in whole or in part, a national, ethnical, racial or religious group, as such,"[73] whether carried out

---

[68] The ICC's jurisdiction may operate in a similar manner with respect to new crimes added by the Assembly of States Parties under the amendment procedures of the Rome Statute. Amendments to add new crimes or change the definitions of those already covered enter into force only for those states parties which have accepted an amendment one year after the deposit of their instruments of ratification or acceptance. The ICC may not exercise its jurisdiction regarding such a crime when committed by nationals of or on the territory of a state party which has not accepted the amendment. The ICC may assert jurisdiction over such crimes committed on the territory of non-party states (or by their nationals) as soon as the amendment enters into force, providing all of the preconditions for jurisdiction are met. See Scheffer, *supra* note 14, at 87.

[69] See Didier Pfirter, The Position of Switzerland with Respect to the ICC Statute and in Particular the Elements of Crimes, 32 CORNELLINT'LL.J. 499, 502 (1999) (describing U.S. proposal and initial resistance to the detailed definition of crimes, which is not standard practice in most legal systems).

[70] See generally William K. Lietzau, *Checks and Balances* and *Elements of Proof: Structural Pillars for the International Criminal Court*, 32 CORNELL INT'L L.J. 477 (1999) (exploring issues surrounding establishment of well-defined elements of crimes).

[71] See id. at 487 (noting that the need for effective mechanisms to enforce criminal law against individuals requires precision and specificity rather than ambiguity and nuance).

[72] Convention on the Prevention and Punishment of Genocide, Dec. 9, 1948, 78 U.N.T.S. 277. See KRIANSAK KITTICHAISAREE, INTERNATIONAL CRIMINAL LAW 69 (2001) (noting that "mobile" groups, such as professions and political groups, are not covered, despite attempts by some delegates at the Rome Conference to include them). [73] *Id.* art. II. Rome Statute art. 6 lists the following acts:

    (a)   Killing members of the group;

in war or during peacetime. The definition is virtually identical to that adopted by Congress in the Genocide Convention Implementation Act of 1987, except that the U.S. Code covers only conduct committed by a U.S. national or conduct committed within the United States.[74]

The victim of genocide is not the individual but the group itself, membership in which is determined automatically by birth rather than by individual choice.[75] The aim must be physical destruction and not merely "cultural genocide," or eliminating the cultural attributes of specific groups, for example, through forced assimilation.[76] To make out a case for genocide, the prosecutor must show that the victim or victims were members of a particular national, ethnic, racial or religious group; the perpetrator intended to destroy that group in whole or in part; and that the perpetrator's conduct (which might include failure to take certain actions[77]) took place in the context of a manifest pattern of similar conduct directed against that group or was conduct that could itself effect such destruction.[78] It is the *mens rea* element that separates genocide from other crimes against humanity: the intent to destroy a group of people as a whole or in significant part.[79]

Crimes against Humanity

The London Charter creating the Nuremberg tribunal was the first codification of the prohibition using the term "crimes against humanity," although the drafters did not treat it as a new concept.[80] There exists no treaty requiring states to prosecute crimes against humanity, but there is

---

(b) Causing serious bodily or mental harm to members of the group;
(c) Deliberately inflicting on the group conditions of life calculated to bring about its physical destruction in whole or in part;
(d) Imposing measures intended to prevent births within the group;
(e) Forcibly transferring children of the group to another group.

[74] Genocide Convention Implementation Act of 1987, Pub. L. No. 100-606, 102 Stat. 3045 (codified at 18 V.S.C. §§ 1091-93).

[75] *See* KRIANGSAK KITTICHAISAREE, INTERNATIONAL CRIMINAL LAW 69 (2001) (noting that "mobile" groups, such as professions and political groups, are not covered, despite attempts by some delegates at the Rome Conference to include them).

[76] *See id.* at 70 (noting forcible transfer of children as a possible exception because the ultimate result is the physical destruction of a named type of group).

[77] Prosecutorv. Jean Kambanda, Case No. ICfR-97-23-S, ICFR T. Ch., Sep.4, 1998 (former Prime Minister of Rwanda guilty of genocide for failing to take action to halt ongoing massacres).

[78] Report of the Preparatory Commission for the International Criminal Court, Part II, Finalized draft text of the Elements of Crimes, U.N. Doc. PCNICC/2000/1/Add.2, Nov. 2, 2000 (hereinafter "Draft Elements").

[79] *See* KITTICHAISAREE, *supra* note 75, at 72-73.

[80] *See id.* at 86.

universal jurisdiction under customary international law to punish as *hostis humani generis* - enemies of mankind - without regard to territorial jurisdiction over a crime or criminal.[81] These crimes include universally condemned acts such as murder, extermination, enslavement, deportation, or religious or political persecution, when carried out as part of a widespread or systematic attack against a civilian population.[82] The distinction between these crimes and war crimes is that they may occur during war or peace and may be perpetrated against stateless victims and persons of the perpetrator's own nationality or that of an allied state.[83] Random crimes would not amount to crimes against humanity; "widespread or systematic" plan or policy does not necessarily connote an intent to destroy a group of people in whole or in part.

The last two elements for each of the crimes against humanity clarify the requisite participation in and knowledge of the systematic plan or attack, but are not intended to be interpreted as requiring proof that the perpetrator had knowledge of all characteristics of the attack or the precise details of the plan or policy of the state or organization.[84] The mental element is satisfied in the case of an emerging attack if the perpetrator intended to further such an attack by any means. The acts need not constitute a military attack. An act perpetrated without constructive or actual knowledge of the existence of the widespread policy or plan would lack the *mens rea* for a crime against humanity. Motive is not relevant.[85]

---

[81] *See* Michael P. Scharf, *Justice Versus Peace, in* THE U.S. AND THE ICC, *supra* note 27, at 179, 185.
[82] Rome Statute art. 7 lists:
  (a) Murder;
  (b) Extermination;
  (c) Enslavement;
  (d) Deportation or forcible transfer of population;
  (e) Imprisonment or other severe deprivation of physical liberty in violation of fundamental rules of international law;
  (f) Torture;
  (g) Rape, sexual slavery, enforced prostitution, forced pregnancy, enforced sterilization, or any other form of sexual violence of comparable gravity;
  (h) Persecution against any identifiable group or collectivity on political, racial, national, ethnic, cultural, religious, gender as defined in paragraph 3, or other grounds that are universally recognized as impermissible under international law, in connection with any act referred to in this paragraph or any crime within the jurisdiction of the Court;
  (i) Enforced disappearance of persons;
  (j) The crime of apartheid;
  (k) Other inhumane acts of a similar character intentionally causing great suffering, or serious injury to body or to mental or physical health.
[83] *See* Scharf, *supra* note 81, at 87.
[84] *See* Draft Elements, *supra* note 78, at 9.
[85] *See* KITTICHAISAREE, *supra* note 75, at 92.

Although there is no U.S. statute codifying crimes against humanity as such, U.S. criminal law prohibits most of the crimes enumerated under the Rome Statute as possible crimes against humanity, as long as they are committed within the United States or by military personnel.[86] Under current law, acts that could constitute crimes against humanity committed by U.S. civilians overseas generally are not triable in U.S. civil or military courts unless they involve torture or certain acts of international terrorism.[87]

War Crimes

War crimes are violations of the international law of war committed during an armed conflict or military occupation,[88] whenever a belligerent "crosses the line" with respect to acceptable combat practices.[89] The Rome statute defines war crimes in art. 8, reiterating war crimes as they are defined in detail in the of Geneva[90] and Hague Conventions,[91] with emphasis on those crimes committed as part of a plan or policy or as part of a large-scale

---

[86] *See* Douglas Cassel, *Empowering United States Courts to Hear Crimes Within* the Jurisdiction of the International Court, 35 NEW ENG. L. REV. 421, 429 (2001).

[87] *See id.* n.39 (listing relevant crimes over which V.S. courts have extraterritorial jurisdiction). Additionally, U.S. courts have jurisdiction to try criminal offenses committed by persons employed by or accompanying the armed forces overseas, or ex-service members who committed a crime overseas, if such crime would be punishable by imprisonment for more than one year if it had committed within the territorial jurisdiction of the United States. 18 U.S.C. § 3261.

[88] *See* Terrorism and the Law of War: Trying Terrorists as War Criminals before Military Commissions, CRS Report RL31191(summary description of sources and contents of the international law of war).

[89] JEAN PICTET, HUMANITARIAN LAW AND THE PROTECTION OF WAR VICTIMS 31 (1975) (describing the principle that "belligerents shall not inflict on their adversaries harm out of proportion to the object of warfare, which is to destroy or weaken the military strength of the enemy").

[90] Geneva Convention for the Amelioration of the Condition of the Wounded and Sick in Armed Forces in the Field, opened for signature Aug. 12, 1949, 6 U.S. T. 3114, T.I.A.S. No. 3362, 75 U.N.T.S. 31 (entered into force Oct. 21, 1950); Geneva Convention for the Amelioration of the Condition of Wounded, Sick and Shipwrecked Members of Armed Forces at Sea, opened for signature Aug. 12, 1949,6 U.S.T. 3217, T.I.A.S. No. 3363, 75 U.N.T.S. 85 (entered into force Oct. 21, 1950); Geneva Convention Relative to the Treatment of Prisoners of War, opened for signature Aug. 12, 1949,6 U.S.T. 3316, T.I.A.S. No. 3364,75 U.N.T.S. 135 (entered into force Oct. 21, 1950)[hereinafter "GPW"]; Geneva Convention Relative to the Protection of Civilian Persons in Time of War, opened for signature Aug. 12, 1949, 6 U.S.T. 3516, T.I.A.S. No. 3365, 75 U.N.T.S. 287 (entered into force Oct. 21, 1950) [hereinafter referred to collectively as the "1949 (Conventions)" or "Conventions"].

[91] Hague Convention No. IV Respecting the Laws and Customs of War on Land, Oct. 18, 1907,36 Stat. 2277, 205 Consol. T.S. 277.

commission of such crimes.⁹² States that are parties to the treaty have the right under Article 124 to opt out of the ICC's jurisdiction with respect to war crimes for a period of seven years.

---

⁹² Rome Statute art. 8(1). Art. 8(2). enumerates the following as war crimes:
- (a)
  - (i) Willful killing;
  - (ii) Torture or inhuman treatment, including biological experiments;
  - (iii) Willfully causing great suffering, or serious injury to body or health;
  - (iv) Extensive destruction and appropriation of property, not justified by military necessity and carried out unlawfully and wantonly;
  - (v) Compelling a prisoner of war or other protected person to serve in the forces of a hostile Power;
  - (vi) Willfully depriving a prisoner of war or other protected person of the rights of fair and regular trial;
  - (vii) Unlawful deportation or transfer or unlawful confinement; (viii) Taking of hostages.
- (b) Other serious violations of the laws and customs applicable in international armed conflict, within the established framework of international law, namely, any of the following acts:
  - (i) Intentionally directing attacks against the civilian population as such or against individual civilians not taking direct part in hostilities;
  - (ii) Intentionally directing attacks against civilian objects, that is, objects which are not military objectives;
  - (iii) Intentionally directing attacks against personnel, installations, material, units or vehicles involved in a humanitarian assistance or peacekeeping mission in accordance with the Charter of the United Nations, as long as they are entitled to the protection given to civilians or civilian objects under the international law of armed conflict;
  - (iv) Intentionally launching an attack in the knowledge that such attack will cause incidental loss of life or injury to civilians or damage to civilian objects or widespread, long-term and severe damage to the natural environment which would be clearly excessive in relation to the concrete and direct overall military advantage anticipated;
  - (v) Attacking or bombarding, by whatever means, towns, villages, dwellings or buildings which are undefended and which are not military objectives;
  - (vi) Killing or wounding a combatant who, having laid down his arms or having no longer means of defense, has surrendered at discretion;
  - (vii) Making improper use of a flag of truce, of the flag or of the military insignia and uniform of the enemy or of the United Nations, as well as of the distinctive emblems of the Geneva Conventions, resulting in death or serious personal injury;
  - (viii) The transfer, directly or indirectly, by the Occupying Power of parts of its own ... civilian population into the territory it occupies, or the deportation or transfer of all or parts of the population of the occupied territory within or outside this territory;
  - (ix) Intentionally directing attacks against buildings dedicated to religion, education, art, science or charitable purposes, historic monuments, hospitals and places where the sick and wounded are collected, provided they are not military objectives;
  - (x) Subjecting persons who are in the power of an adverse party to physical mutilation or to medical or scientific experiments of any kind which are neither justified by the medical, dental or hospital treatment of the person

	concerned nor carried out in his or her interest, and which cause death to or seriously endanger the health of such person or persons;
(xi)	Killing or wounding treacherously individuals belonging to the hostile nation or army;
(xii)	Declaring that no quarter will be given;
(xiii)	Destroying or seizing the enemy's property unless such destruction or seizure be imperatively demanded by the necessities of war;
(xiv)	Declaring abolished, suspended or inadmissible in a court of law the rights and actions of the nationals of the hostile party;
(xv)	Compelling the nationals of the hostile party to take part in the operations of war directed against their own country, even if they were in the belligerent's service before the commencement of the war;
(xvi)	Pillaging a town or place, even when taken by assault;
(xvii)	Employing poison or poisoned weapons;
(xviii)	Employing asphyxiating, poisonous or other gases, and all analogous liquids, materials or devices;
(xix)	Employing bullets which expand or flatten easily in the human body, such as bullets with a hard envelope which does not entirely cover the core or is pierced with incisions;
(xx)	Employing weapons, projectiles and material and methods of warfare which are of a nature to cause superfluous injury or unnecessary suffering or which are inherently indiscriminate in violation of the international law of armed conflict, provided that such weapons, projectiles and material and methods of warfare are the subject of a comprehensive prohibition and are included in an annex to this Statute, by an
(xxi)	amendment in accordance with the relevant provisions set forth in articles 121 and 123;
(xxii)	Committing outrages upon personal dignity, in particular humiliating and degrading treatment;
(xxiii)	Committing rape, sexual slavery, enforced prostitution, forced pregnancy, as defined in article/, paragraph 2(f), enforced sterilization, or any other form of sexual violence also constituting a grave breach of the Geneva Conventions;
(xxiv)	Utilizing the presence of a civilian or other protected person to render certain points, areas or military forces immune from military operations;
(xxv)	Intentionally directing attacks against buildings, material, medical units and transport, and personnel using the distinctive emblems of the Geneva Conventions in conformity with international law;
(xxvi)	Intentionally using starvation of civilians as a method of warfare by depriving them of objects indispensable to their survival, including willfully impeding relief supplies as provided for under the Geneva Conventions;
(xxvii)	Conscripting or enlisting children under the age of fifteen years into the national armed forces or using them to participate actively in hostilities.

(c) In the case of an armed conflict not of an international character, serious violations of article 3 common to the four Geneva Conventions of 12 August 1949, namely, any of the following acts committed against persons taking no active part in the hostilities, including members of armed forces who have laid down their arms and those placed hors de combat by sickness, wounds, detention or any other cause:
  (i) Violence to life and person, in particular murder of all kinds, mutilation, cruel treatment and torture;
  (ii) Committing outrages upon personal dignity, in particular humiliating and degrading treatment;
  (iii) Taking of hostages;

The prosecutor must show that the crimes took place in the context of an armed conflict, that the perpetrator was aware of those circumstances, and that the perpetrator was aware that the victim had protected status under the

---

      (iv) The passing of sentences and the carrying out of executions without previous judgment pronounced by a regularly constituted court, affording all judicial guarantees which are generally recognized as indispensable.
- (d) Paragraph 2(c) applies to armed conflicts not of an international character and thus does not apply to situations of internal disturbances and tensions, such as riots, isolated and sporadic acts of violence or other acts of a similar nature.
- (e) Other serious violations of the laws and customs applicable in armed conflicts not of an international character, within the established framework of international law, namely, any of the following acts:
  - (i) Intentionally directing attacks against the civilian population as such or against individual civilians not taking direct part in hostilities;
  - (ii) Intentionally directing attacks against buildings, material, medical units and transport, and personnel using the distinctive emblems of the Geneva Conventions in conformity with international law;
  - (iii) Intentionally directing attacks against personnel, installations, material, units or vehicles involved in a humanitarian assistance or peacekeeping mission in accordance with the Charter of the United Nations, as long as they are entitled to the protection given to civilians or civilian objects under the law of armed conflict;
  - (iv) Intentionally directing attacks against buildings dedicated to religion, education, art, science or charitable purposes, historic monuments, hospitals and places where the sick and wounded are collected, provided they are not military objectives;
  - (v) Pillaging a town or place, even when taken by assault; (vi) Committing rape, sexual slavery, enforced prostitution, forced pregnancy, as defined in article 7, paragraph 2 (f), enforced sterilization, and any other form of sexual violence also constituting a serious violation of article 3 common to the four Geneva Conventions;
  - (vi) Conscripting or enlisting children under the age of fifteen years into armed forces or groups or using them to participate actively in hostilities;
  - (vii) Ordering the displacement of the civilian population for reasons related to the conflict, unless the security of the civilians involved or imperative military reasons so demand;
  - (viii) Killing or wounding treacherously a combatant adversary;
  - (ix) Declaring that no quarter will be given;
  - (x) Subjecting persons who are in the power of another party to the conflict to physical mutilation or to medical or scientific experiments of any kind which are neither justified by the medical, dental or hospital treatment of the person concerned nor carried out in his or her interest, and which cause death to or seriously endanger the health of such person or persons;
  - (xi) Destroying or seizing the property of an adversary unless such destruction or seizure be imperatively demanded by the necessities of the conflict;
- (f) Paragraph 2(e) applies to armed conflicts not of an international character and thus does not apply to situations of internal disturbances and tensions, such as riots, isolated and sporadic acts of violence or other acts of a similar nature. It applies to armed conflicts that take place in the territory of a State when there is protracted armed conflict between governmental authorities and organized armed groups or between such groups.

Geneva Conventions or Protocols.[93] There is no need to show that the act was committed as part of a widespread series of violations.[94]

The War Crimes Act of 1996[95] establishes U.S. federal jurisdiction to punish war crimes, as defined in international treaties to which the United States is a party, when perpetrated by or against U.S. nationals. U.S. service members and others may also be tried by courts-martial or military commission for acts in violation of the law of war;[96] ordinarily, U.S. practice is to try U.S. service members by court-martial rather than in federal court for offenses against the law of war.[97]

Aggression

The Rome Conference Delegates included "aggression" among the crimes over which the ICC would have jurisdiction, but were unable to reach an agreement to adopt a definition.[98] Instead, the Conferees agreed to work toward establishing a definition after the Rome Statute enters into force. The ICC will be able to exercise jurisdiction over the crime of aggression only after such a provision has been adopted and entered into force for the relevant state party.

---

[93] *See* Draft Elements, *supra* note 78, at 18.
[94] Rome Statute art. 8(1)([The ICC has jurisdiction over war crimes] *"in particular* when committed as a part of a plan or policy or as part of a large-scale commission of such crimes."(emphasis added)). According to the Draft Elements, "elements for war crimes under . . . [the Rome] Statute shall be interpreted within the established framework of the international law of armed conflict " *See* Draft Elements, *supra* note 78, at 18. International law does not appear to require proof of the existence of any policy, official or unofficial, to commit a war crime. *See* Kriangsak Kittichaisaree, *The NATO Military Action and the Potential Impact of the International Criminal Court,* 4 SING. J. INT'L & COMP. L. 498,517 (2000). The "in particular" language is meant to serve as a jurisdictional threshold to prevent the ICC from taking up relatively insignificant cases. *See id.* Critics have argued, however, that this threshold is still too low, increasing the likelihood of prosecution of members of the armed forces. See Jimmy Gurule, United States Opposition to the 1998 Rome Statute Establishing an International Criminal Court: *Is the Court's Jurisdiction Truly Complementary to National Criminal Jurisdictions?,* 35 CORNELL INT'LL.J.1, 30-31 (2002).
[95] 18 U.S.C. § 2441.
[96] Article 18 of the UCMJ, 10 U.S.C. § 818, provides general court martial jurisdiction over "any person who by the law of war is subject to trial by a military tribunal and may adjudge any punishment permitted by the law of war." UCMJ art. 21,10 U.S.C. § 821, provides that court-martial jurisdiction does not deprive military commissions of jurisdiction to try any person for such crimes.
[97] *See* Department of the Army, FM 27-10, THE LAW OF LAND WARFARE para. 507 (1956).

Although there were trials for aggression at Nuremberg,[99] an acceptable definition for its elements has long eluded the international community, impeding earlier attempts to establish an international criminal court.[100] Article 39 of the U.N. Charter leaves it to the Security Council to determine the existence of and take action with respect to "any threat to the peace, breach of the peace, or act of aggression."[101] Aggression is not defined in the U.N. Charter, however, because it was reportedly feared that advances in weapons and techniques of modern warfare would make the definition impractical and subject to manipulation, and might cause the Security Council to take premature action.[102] The U.N. General Assembly adopted a resolution in 1974[103] addressing the definition of aggression, but it has only been invoked once by the Security Council, to declare South Mica guilty of aggression against Angola.[104] The definition contains an enumeration of offenses included as possible aggression, but leaves the determination to the Security Council.[105]

Any definition of aggression adopted for the ICC must "be consistent with the relevant provisions of the Charter of the United Nations."[106] If this provision is interpreted to include a determination by the Security Council that an act of aggression has been committed in the definition for aggression under the Rome Statute, then the United States and NATO likely need not fear prosecution for acts of aggression.[107] On the other hand, some observers have expressed concern that the Rome Statute can be used to divest the Security Council of its prerogative in determining whether an act of aggression has occurred, allowing legitimate acts of self-defense to be punished as aggression.[108] Such a result could, they argue, curtail the U.S.' options for using military force for valid reasons.

---

[98] See generally Silvia A. Fernandez de Gurmendi, The Working Group on Aggression at the Preparatory Commission for the International Criminal Court, 25 FORDHAM INT'L L.J. 589 (2002).
[99] See id. at 592 (discussing World War II precedents for charging persons with aggression).
[100] See Gurule, supra note 94, at 2.
[101] U.N. Charter art. 39.
[102] See Kittichaisaree, supra note 94, at 504.
[103] U.N. GAOR, Supp. No. 19, U.N. Doc A/9615 (1974).
[104] See Kitticbaisaree, supra note 94, at 505 (citing U.N. Security Council Resolution 418 of 4 Nov. 1977).
[105] See id. at 504-05.
[106] Rome Statute art. 5(2).
[107] See Kittichaisaree, supra note 94, at 506 (predicting that "NATO members who are also Permanent Members of the Security Council would certainly veto any draft Security Council Resolution determining that an act of aggression has been committed by NATO").
[108] See Scheffer, supra note 14, at 83 (advocating U.S. involvement in the ICC to avoid a "definition of "aggression" that does not include a determination by the U.N. Security Council).

JURISDICTION OVER PERSONS

It is widely accepted that the above crimes enumerated in the Statute are subject to universal jurisdiction under international law;[109] that is, any nation may lawfully try any individual accused of such crimes in its domestic court system without regard to the nationality of the alleged perpetrator or the territory where the crime is alleged to have taken place.[110] In practice, however, political realities appear often to have precluded nations from asserting jurisdiction over suspected war criminals,[111] allowing many of them to enjoy impunity for their alleged crimes. The ICC is intended to resolve the problem of in1punity for perpetrators of atrocities,[112] but has led to a different concern, namely, that the ICC may be used by some countries to make trumped-up allegations accusing other states' policymakers, or even implementors of disfavored policies, of engaging in criminal conduct. Probably the most divisive issue at the Rome Conference was the effort to reach a balance between the two extremes - how to bring perpetrators of atrocities to justice while protecting innocent persons from frivolous prosecution and unjust punishment. The conferees finally adopted a somewhat complex system of triggering mechanisms to control how cases were to be referred to the ICC for possible prosecution.

---

[109] The Geneva Conventions require signatory nations to enact domestic legislation to punish perpetrators of grave breaches of the Conventions, and to actively investigate such crimes, and prosecute or extradite the alleged perpetrators. *See* GPW, *supra* note 90, art. 129. Other treaties with similar clauses include the Conventions on Hijacking and Aircraft Sabotage, as well as most other conventions against terrorism. *See* Michael P. Scharf, *Universal Jurisdiction: Myths, Realities, and Prospects: Application of Treaty-based Universal Jurisdiction to Nationals of Non-Party Status*, 35 NEW ENG.L. REV. 363 (2001). *But see* Casey, *supra* note 62, at 855 (disputing the validity of universal jurisdiction). For an in-depth analysis on the applicability of universal jurisdiction to various crimes under international law, see generally Bassiouni, *supra* note 23.

[110] This concept is distinct from domestic jurisdiction. For example, although there is universal jurisdiction over grave breaches of the Geneva Conventions, U.S. law only allows prosecution of such crimes in its federal courts where the victim or perpetrator is a U.S. national. *See generally* Cassel, *supra* note 86 (recommending changes in U.S. law to fully encompass crimes over which the ICC will have jurisdiction); 18 U.S.C. § 2441 (War Crimes Act).

[111] *See* Bassiouni, *supra* note 23, at 136 (concluding that state practice does not support the assertion that universal jurisdiction has reached the level of customary international law in all cases where it has been claimed).

[112] Rome Statute preamble (declaring signatory states are "[d]etermined to put an end to impunity for the perpetrators of these crimes and thus to contribute to the prevention of such crimes").

Although the ICC's jurisdiction over the class of suspected criminals is based on the concept of universal jurisdiction for the covered crimes,[113] the ICC may not establish jurisdiction over accused persons unless certain preconditions are met. First, unless a case has been referred to the ICC by the U.N. Security Council, the ICC's jurisdiction is complementary to that of national courts: the ICC will try cases only when the state with custody of the accused is unable or unwilling genuinely to prosecute.[114] Where that is determined to be the case, the ICC may take jurisdiction if either the state on whose territory the conduct occurred or the state of nationality of the person accused is a party to the Rome Statute or consents to the jurisdiction of the ICC.

TRIGGERING MECHANISMS.

There are three avenues through which cases may be referred to the ICC. Either a state party to the Statute, the ICC prosecutor, or the U.N. Security Council[115] may refer cases to the ICC, in accordance with corresponding articles of the Statute. The Security Council may also defer an investigation referred by a state or the prosecutor for a renewable period of 12 months by adopting a resolution under Chapter VII of the U.N. Charter to that effect.[116] During the negotiations, the United States sought a more powerful role for the Security Council, in which any permanent member would be able to veto a referral. The conferees ultimately rejected this proposal because it was seen to re-introduce political considerations to the prosecutions that are perceived to be responsible for the phenomenon of impunity the ICC is intended to avoid. The Statute as finally adopted allows a single permanent member of the Security Council to veto a *deferral,* allowing the Prosecutor to move forward with a case. With the support of the Permanent Five and four other members of the Security Council, the provision could allow the ICC's exercise of jurisdiction to be forestalled indefinitely.

---

[113] *Id.* ("Recalling that it is the duty of every State to exercise its criminal jurisdiction over those responsible for international crimes"); *see* Jordan Faust, *The Reach of ICC Jurisdiction Over Non-Signatory Nationals,* 33 VAND. J. TRANSNAT'L L. 1, 7 (2000) (describing ICC jurisdiction as a "form of limited universal jurisdiction").

[114] Rome Statute art. 17. *See* van der Vyver, *supra* note 20, at 2-3 (describing principle of complementarity and the possible questions it raises regarding state sovereignty in any determination of "unwillingness to prosecute").

[115] Rome Statute art. 13 states that the U.N. Security Council may recommend investigation of alleged crimes using its authority under chapter VII of the U.N. Charter.

[116] *Id.* art. 16.

Referral by a State Party

A state party to the ICC may refer a "situation" to the Prosecutor for investigation where it appears that one or more crimes under the jurisdiction of the ICC have been committed.[117] The referral must be made in writing,[118] and as far as possible, must specify the relevant circumstances and be accompanied by all of the supporting documentation available to the referring state.[119] There is no requirement that the referring state have territorial jurisdiction to prosecute the crime or custody of the alleged perpetrators. If the Prosecutor determines there is sufficient cause to commence an investigation, he or she must notify all states parties and any other state that would normally be able to assert jurisdiction over the crime, possibly on a confidential basis and taking measures to preserve evidence or prevent the absconding of persons.[120]

If a state with conventional jurisdiction notifies the Prosecutor within one month of its intent to investigate the crime, the Prosecutor must defer to that state, but may make an application to the Trial Chamber to commence an investigation on the basis that the state's investigation is not "genuine."[121] The Prosecutor may request the state to provide periodic status reports on the investigation. The decision as to whether a state is "unwilling or unable genuinely" to carry out its investigation is determined by the Pre-Trial Chamber. The state must be informed that the Prosecutor intends to challenge a state's intent or ability to investigate, allowing sufficient time for the state to prepare to present evidence on its behalf. The state may challenge the determination to the Appeals Chamber, and if that challenge is unsuccessful, may later bring a challenge to the admissibility of the case under article 19, providing there are additional facts or a significant change of circumstances.

In the event the Prosecutor decides not to initiate an investigation, the referring state may request a review before the Pre-Trial Chamber,[122] which may request the Prosecutor to reconsider the decision within ninety days following notification.[123] The Pre-Trial Chamber may conduct a review of the Prosecutor's decision on its own motion if the decision is based on the Prosecutor's determination that a prosecution is not in the interest of justice

---

[117] *Id.* art. 14.
[118] Draft RPE 45.
[119] Rome Statute art. 14(2).
[120] *Id.* art. 18(1).
[121] *Id.* art. 18(2-5).
[122] *Id.* art. 53.
[123] Draft RPE 107.

as specified in paragraphs l(c) or 2(c) of article 53. The decision of the Pre-Trial Chamber in this case is controlling. If new information or evidence becomes available after the Prosecutor has decided not to investigate or if the Pre-Trial Chamber does not authorize an investigation, the Prosecutor may initiate a new investigation.[124]

Initiation by Prosecutor

If the Prosecutor becomes aware of possible crimes within the jurisdiction of the ICC, he or she may commence self-initiated investigation. There does not appear to be any limitation on how the Prosecutor receives the information or who can submit it. The Prosecutor may request information from states, non-governmental organizations (NGOs), or any other reliable source as deemed appropriate, and must protect the confidentiality of all such information in accordance with the Rome Statute and Rules of Procedure and Evidence.[125] If the Prosecutor concludes that there is a "reasonable basis" for an investigation in a given situation, he or she must first submit a request to the Pre-Trial Chamber for authorization to proceed. The Chamber, in turn, must determine both that there is a "reasonable basis" to proceed with an investigation and that "the case appears to fall within the jurisdiction of the Court." Victims may make presentations to the Pre-Trial Chamber, but there does not appear to be an opportunity for a state with jurisdiction to intercede at this juncture. Once the investigation is authorized, the Prosecutor must notify relevant parties as in the case of a referral by a state party.[126] At that time, a state with jurisdiction over the crime may submit its request for deferral.

If the Prosecutor determines that sufficient basis for an investigation does not exist, he or she must inform those who provided the information,[127] but there is no opportunity for the referring persons or entities to challenge the decision. However, the Pre-Trial Chamber may initiate its own review, giving the Prosecutor a deadline for the submission of observations.[128]

As noted above, the U.N. Security Council may issue a stay preventing the Prosecutor from proceeding in cases submitted by states parties or initiated by the Prosecutor. There does not appear to be a provision in the Rome Statute or Draft RPE stating when, if ever, any organ of the ICC is

---

[124] Rome Statute arts. 15 and 53(4).
[125] Draft RPE 46.
[126] Rome Statute art. 18(1).
[127] *Id.* art. 15(6).

required to inform the Security Council of an investigation under consideration. Moreover, before the Security Council can act under Chapter VII of the U.N. Charter, as required to defer an investigation under art. 16 of the Rome Statute, the Council must first determine there is "a threat to the peace, breach of the peace or act of aggression. . . ."[129]

Referral by the U.N. Security Council

One of the reasons for initiating an international criminal court was to give the Security Council a permanent forum for war crimes trials, without necessitating the intense effort required to set up an *ad hoc* tribunal. The Security Council may thus, pursuant to its mandate under Chapter VII of the U.N. Charter, refer a case to the Prosecutor for investigation.[130] Presumably, however, the U.N. Security Council is not precluded from initiating a separate *ad hoc* tribunal if for some reason it were to determine that the ICC would be unable to conduct a fair and effective trial, although some predict that the ICC will bring an end to the use of such tribunals.[131]

Once the Prosecutor receives a referral by the U.N. Security Council, he or she determines whether or not an investigation is warranted using the same procedure as in the case of any other type of referral. The Security Council may request that the Pre-Trial Chamber review a decision of the Prosecutor not to initiate an investigation, but may not *require* the Prosecutor to proceed. The most important difference between a referral by the Security Council and the other types of referrals is that the consent of neither the state of nationality of the accused nor the state on whose territory the crime was committed is necessary for the ICC to assert its jurisdiction. The Prosecutor need not inform states with jurisdiction in accordance with art.18, in order to give such states the opportunity to request deferral; however, it appears that those states retain the right to contest the jurisdiction of the ICC based on complementarity.

---

[128] Draft RPE 109.
[129] U.N. Charter art. 39. *See* Gurule, *supra* note 94, at 22 (criticizing Rome Statute art. 16 for perceived weaknesses).
[130] Rome Statute art. 13(b).
[131] See Mark A. Summers, *A Fresh Look at the Jurisdictional Provisions of the Statute of the International Criminal Court: the Case for Scrapping the Treaty*, 20 WIS. INT'L L.J. 57,75 (2001); Michael P. Scharf, *The United States and the International Criminal Court: A Recommendation for the Bush Administration*, & ISLA J INT'L & COMP. L. 385, 387 (2002).

ICC JURISDICTION OVER CITIZENS OF NON-PARTIES.

The above-outlined triggering mechanisms for jurisdiction of the ICC make it possible for the ICC to investigate and try citizens of states that have not signed or ratified the Rome Statute. Thus, under certain circumstances the ICC could exercise jurisdiction over a U.S. citizen accused of one or more of the crimes specified in the treaty, even if the United States does not ratify it. If the United States voluntarily consents to the exercise of ICC jurisdiction, or if the state on whose territory an American citizen has allegedly committed the crime consents, the ICC could try a case despite the fact that neither state has ratified the treaty.[132] If an American citizen is accused of committing one of the covered crimes on the territory of a state party, consent is automatic on the part of the territorial state, but either state can supercede the ICC's jurisdiction by undertaking to prosecute the crime in its domestic courts.

Thus, U.S. nationals could be subject to investigation and trial by the ICC if the country in which the alleged crime occurred is either a party to the Rome Statute or consents to the ICC's jurisdiction, and has or is able to gain custody of the alleged U.S. offender. This possibility appears to exist mainly with respect to U.S. military personnel stationed or found in such a country. It also appears to exist with respect to U.S. public officials whose actions are alleged to have caused one of the crimes designated in the Rome Statute, should that official be found in (or extradited to) the country where the crime allegedly occurred.[133] Such exercises of jurisdiction over U.S. nationals could occur pursuant to the initiative of the state where the crime allegedly occurred or of the Prosecutor.[134]

Given the nature of acts covered as crimes that can be prosecuted by the ICC, it is thought to be a rare situation in which an American citizen acting in his or her own capacity could commit such a crime. Americans who are not service members or government officials could, at present, presumably fall under the jurisdiction of the ICC only if they participate in insurgencies abroad or commit any of the covered acts on behalf of a foreign government

---

[132] Rome Statute art. 13.
[133] The Rome Statute makes military commanders criminally responsible for the acts of forces under "his or her effective command and control." It also eliminates all immunities "based on official capacity." *Id.* arts. 28 and 27, respectively.
[134] *Id.* art. 13. The concurrence of the state in which the crime took place would be necessary for the ICC to maintain its jurisdiction. The ICC can also exercise its jurisdiction pursuant to a referral from the Security Council, whether or not the state of nationality or territoriality concurs. Because the U.S. possesses a veto in the Security Council, such a referral could only occur if the U.S. consented.

or entity. If the United States is able to and does assert jurisdiction over the crime and the accused, the ICC could not proceed with prosecution unless it were to find the United States unwilling or unable genuinely to investigate or prosecute the crime. If another country has jurisdiction and decides to surrender a U.S. person accused of a covered crime to the ICC, the United States could appeal the jurisdiction of the ICC.[135]

If the jurisdiction of the ICC eventually is expanded to include terrorism and drug trafficking, there is arguably a greater probability that Americans abroad could be tried by the ICC, as those crimes may not require as a prerequisite a showing that they are part of a greater scheme. However, it has been noted, Americans abroad who are accused of perpetrating a terrorist act or engaging in illicit drug trade are subject to the laws and legal system of the country where the crime took place, without regard to whether the United States consents to such jurisdiction. Some observers have raised the possibility, therefore, that in such cases accused Americans could conceivably enjoy more comprehensive procedural due process rights before the ICC than they would receive in the domestic courts of some foreign states.

COMPLEMENTARITY AND OTHER CHALLENGES TO JURISDICTION

According to Article 17 of the Rome Statute, the ICC must find it has no jurisdiction where a state with jurisdiction is investigating or prosecuting the crime, or has investigated the case and genuinely determined that prosecution of the person is unwarranted.[136] The ICC shall determine a case

---

[135] Such country would also have the option of trying the case in its own courts or extraditing the prisoner to the United States. The Rome Statute provides that states parties who receive a request for surrender from the ICC and a :request for extradition from a non-party state, with which it has an extradition treaty or the like, shall decide which course to take based on the dates of the requests, the interest of the requesting state in prosecuting the crime, and the possibility of subsequent surrender of the person between the ICC and the non-party state. Rome Statute art. 19. If there is no obligation to extradite, the requested state should give priority to the ICC. *Id.* Under Article 98 of the Rome Statute, the ICC may not proceed with a request for surrender or assistance which would require the requested state to act inconsistently with its obligations under international law regarding state or diplomatic immunity or an agreement not to surrender the country's national to the ICC unless the ICC gains the cooperation of that third state. It is unclear whether a treaty violation that results in the ICC's custody of an accused is grounds for challenging the ICC's jurisdiction, either by the accused or the state of nationality of the accused.

[136] *See* Rome Statute art. 17. Paragraph 1 provides the ICC shall determine a case is inadmissible where:

is inadmissible if the accused has already stood trial for the conduct unless it determines the trial was conducted solely for the purpose of shielding the individual from prosecution by the ICC or if it was otherwise conducted in a manner "inconsistent with an intent to bring the person concerned to justice."[137] In order to give the appropriate states the opportunity to take charge of a given situation, the Prosecutor is required to inform all states parties and other interested states when there is a "reasonable basis to commence an investigation" (except in cases referred by the Security Council).[138]

The United States may thus challenge the ICC's jurisdiction over its national in a preliminary proceeding on the basis that it is willing and able to undertake investigation itself. The Statute also provides that a state "from which acceptance of jurisdiction is required under article 12" may challenge the court's jurisdiction.[139] Presumably, the United States could challenge the ICC's jurisdiction over a crime allegedly committed by its national even if no U.S. court has jurisdiction over the crime, by challenging one of the other prerequisites for admissibility of the case. For example, the United States could argue the gravity of the crime of which its national is accused is not sufficiently severe to warrant a trial at the ICC, or that the crime is merely an isolated incident and not part of a larger campaign as required for covered crimes.[140]

(a) The case is being investigated or prosecuted by a State which has jurisdiction over it, unless the State is unwilling or unable genuinely to carry out the investigation or prosecution;
(b) The case has been investigated by a State which has jurisdiction over it and the State has decided not to prosecute the person concerned, unless the decision resulted from the unwillingness or inability of the State genuinely to prosecute;
(c) The person concerned has already been tried for conduct which is the subject of the complaint, and a trial by the Court is not permitted under article 20, paragraph 3;
(d) The case is not of sufficient gravity to justify further action by the Court.

[137] *Id.* art. 20.
[138] *Id.* art. 18. A state has one month after receipt of the notification to advise the ICC that it is investigating (or has investigated) the situation. The Prosecutor must then defer, unless he or she obtains an authorization to investigate from a Pre-Trial Chamber.
[139] Presumably this language refers to both the state where a crime allegedly occurred and the state whose national allegedly perpetrated it, even though the acceptance of only one of them is *required* for the ICC to find jurisdiction.
[140] *See* Finalized Draft Text of the Elements of Crimes, Report of the Preparatory Commission for the International Criminal Court, PCNICC/2000/1 (2000), *available at* http://www.un.org/law/icc/statute/elements/elemfra.htm. As currently defined, genocide crimes have as an element that the "conduct took place in the context of a manifest pattern of similar conduct directed against [the target] group or was conduct that could itself effect such destruction." Crimes against humanity include the elements that the conduct was committed with knowledge or intent that it contribute to a "widespread or systematic attack directed against a civilian population." *See id.* at 9. War Crimes listed under paragraphs (a) and (b) of Article 8 of the Rome Statute apply to situations of international armed conflict and incorporate the

Thus, many supporters of the Rome Statute believe that the principle of complementarity, properly applied, is sufficient to insulate U.S. service members and civilians from prosecution at the ICC. After all, they argue, it is virtually inconceivable that the American judicial system will suffer such a massive breakdown as one that would render it "unable to obtain the accused or the necessary evidence and testimony or otherwise unable to carry out its proceedings."[141] Neither is it likely that the United States would be unwilling to investigate alleged atrocities committed by its own troops or officials abroad.[142] Some have suggested that changes in U.S. statutes to broaden the jurisdiction of federal courts to cover all crimes over which the ICC might assert jurisdiction could enhance the implementation of complementarity by precluding a finding by the ICC that the United States is "unable" to prosecute one of its citizens.[143] Opponents of the ICC, however, question whether complementarity will operate as promised, or whether the ICC judges will focus on a perceived deficiency in U.S. trial or court-martial practice to declare that a particular U.S. prosecution or investigation was not conducted in a manner consistent with "the intent to bring the person concerned to justice."[144]

Thus, the primary issue regarding complementarity is the extent to which the ICC will defer to national decisions regarding the handling of purported crimes under the jurisdiction of the ICC. It is unclear, for example, whether the ICC would defer to a decision by a nation to constitute a truth and reconciliation commission, where such a commission could grant amnesty to the perpetrators of genocide in exchange for a full accounting of the events underlying the charge. The granting of amnesty is arguably contrary to the intent to bring criminals to justice, but a nation recovering

---

Geneva Conventions of 1949. Paragraph 2(e) applies to armed conflicts not of an international character and explicitly excludes "internal disturbances and tensions, such as riots, isolated and sporadic acts of violence or other acts of a similar nature." There must be "protracted armed conflict between governmental authorities and organized armed groups or between such groups" before any conduct can be considered a war crime under that paragraph.

[141] Rome Statute art. 12. *See* Ruth Wedgwood, *The Constitution and the FCC in* THE U.S. AND THE ICC, *supra* note 27, at 119, 127.

[142] *See id.* at 127.

[143] *See* Cassel, *supra* note 86, at 437; Robinson O. Everett, American Service members and the ICC, in THE US AND THE ICC, *supra* note 27, at 137, 142.

[144] Rome Statute art. 12(2(c»). *See* Gurule, *Supra* note 94, at 27-28 (arguing that the ICC's jurisdiction is not truly complementary because the Rome Statute allows the ICC to second-guess the decisions of national courts).

from the effects of genocide might find it in its interest to form such a commission rather than try to prosecute the alleged perpetrators.[145]

---

[145] *See generally* Michael P. Scharf, *Justice versus Peace, in* THE U.S. AND THE ICC, *supra* note 27, at 179.

Chapter 4

RULES OF PROCEDURE AND EVIDENCE

The Rome Statute contains a comprehensive set of procedural safeguards for the rights of the accused. While some legal experts agree that the Rome Statute contains "the most comprehensive list of due process protections which has so far been promulgated,"[146] some of the ICC's detractors maintain that the procedures nevertheless fall short of U.S. constitutional standards of due process.[147] Some observers caution that the attempt to create a hybrid set of rules, mixing ideas from the common law and civil law traditions, may lead to unpredictable and possibly unjust results.[148]

The Preparatory Commission completed its draft of the Rules of Procedure and Evidence[149] at its Fifth Session in June of 2000. These rules implement and embellish the procedural aspects of the Rome Statute, and are subject to approval by the Assembly of States Parties at its first meeting. A summary comparison of some procedural safeguards in the Rome Statute and those mandated by the U.S. Constitution is set out below.[150]

---

[146] See, e.g., The International Criminal Court: Hearing before the House Comm. on International Relations, 106th Cong. 92-101, 96 (2000) (statement of Monroe Leigh on behalf of the American Bar Association); Scheffer, supra note 14, at 94; Wedgwood, supra note 141, at 123.

[147] See, e.g. Casey, supra note 62.

[148] See generally Robert Christensen, Getting to Peace by Reconciling Notions of Justice: The Importance of Considering Discrepancies Between Civil and Common Legal Systems in the Formation of the International Criminal Court, 6 UCLA J INT'LL. & FOREIGN AFF. 391 (2001).

[149] Draft RPE, *supra* note 57.

[150] For a brief comparison of ICC procedural safeguards to federal and military rules of procedure and evidence in chart form, see Selected Procedural Safeguards in Federal, Military, and International Courts, CRS Report RL31262. Of course, just as the U.S. Constitution is interpreted in large measure through case law, the Rome Statute may be

THE RIGHT TO A JURY TRIAL

The Rome Statute does not provide for trial by jury; instead, it follows the civil law tradition of employing a panel of judges to decide questions of both fact and law. This issue does not appear to have been a major point of contention for U.S. participants during the negotiations of the Rome Statute. This may be true because the Americans considered most at risk, U.S. service members, are subject to court martial under the Uniform Code of Military Justice (UCMJ) and are not entitled to trial by civil jury.[151] American civilians who are accused of crimes overseas are subject to the jurisdiction of the country where the crime took place, and may be tried under that country's laws, which in many cases do not include the right to a trial by jury.

Some opponents of the Rome Treaty argue that it would be unconstitutional for the United States to ratify the Rome Statute because U.S. participation in any court that does not provide for a jury trial in cases where the Constitution requires one would be unlawful.[152] The center position to this argument is that the Constitution does not bar trial by military commission without a Jury under certain circumstances,[153] even the trial of American citizens not members of the armed forces.[154] They also note that the United States has participated in international courts previously, even where American citizens could be tried before them.[155] Finally, the Supreme Court has ruled that persons may be extradited to stand trial in a foreign country despite the lack of jury trial and other procedural safeguards that would be available to that same person if tried in U.S. courts.[156]

THE PRESUMPTION OF INNOCENCE

The Rome Statute provides that "[e]veryone shall be presumed to be innocent until proven guilty before the Court."[157] It also places the burden of

---

expected to acquire some new contours in the light of the ICC's interpretation of the Statute as well as case law interpretation.

[151] *See id; Wedgwood, et al., supra note 8, at 130.*
[152] *See Casey, supra note 62, at 861-62.*
[153] *See Wedgwood, supra note 141, at 1~6 (citing Ex parte Quirin, 317 U.S. 1 (1942)).*
[154] *See Madsen v. Kinsella, 343 U.S. 341 (1952)(upholding jurisdiction of military commission to try civilians in occupied foreign territory).*
[155] *See Wedgwood, supra note 141, at 122 (giving as an example the International Criminal Tribunal for the Former Yugoslavia).*
[156] *See id.* at 124 (citing Charleton v. Kelly, 229 U.S. 447 (1913)).
[157] Rome Statute art. 66.

proof on the Prosecutor and sets the standard for a conviction to proof beyond a reasonable doubt.[158] The Prosecutor must first have confirmed by the Pre-Trial Chamber that there are sufficient grounds to believe the accused committed the crime as charged.[159] The accused may object to the charges, challenge the evidence against him, or present his own evidence.[160] Once the Pre-Trial Chamber has confirmed the charges, the case will come before a Trial Chamber, which must ensure the accused understands the nature of the charges and then allow the accused to enter a plea of innocence or make an admission of guilt.[161] If the accused has admitted guilt, the Trial Chamber must review the evidence to ensure it is sufficient to support the admission.[162] If the Trial Chamber is not satisfied that the evidence is sufficient, it will proceed with the trial as if the accused entered a plea of innocence.[163] The Trial Chamber is not bound by any plea agreements the Prosecutor may have made with the accused.[164]

In U.S. courts, the accused is entitled to appear in court "without unnecessary physical restraints or other indicia of guilt, such as appearing in prison uniform, that may be prejudicial to the jury."[165] The ICC rules provide that any instruments of restraint "shall be removed when the person appears before a Chamber."[166] The rules do not specify whether military personnel are entitled to appear in uniform before the court.

THE PRIVILEGE AGAINST COMPELLED SELF-INCRIMINATION

During an investigation, if there is reason to believe a person has committed a crime under the jurisdiction of the ICC, that person has the right "[t]o remain silent, without such silence being a consideration in the

---

[158] *Id.*
[159] *Id.* art. 61.
[160] *Id.* art. 61(6).
[161] *Id.* art. 64(8).
[162] *Id.* art. 65.
[163] *Id.* art. 65(3).
[164] *Id.* art. 65(5).
[165] SeeHolbrook v. Flynn, 475 U.S. 560 (1986). A similar rule applies to courts-martial. *See* Manual for Courts Martial (M.C.M.), established as Exec. Order No. 12473,49 Fed. Reg 17,152, (Apr. 23, 1984). Rules for Courts-Martial (R.C.M.) Rule. 804 provides that "[t]he accused shall be properly attired in uniform with grade insignia and any decorations to which entitled. Physical restraint shall not be imposed unless prescribed by the military judge."
[166] Draft RPE 121

determination of guilt or innocence."[167] Any individual questioned during an investigation "[s]hall not be compelled to incriminate himself or herself or to confess guilt; [and s]hall not be subjected to any form of coercion, duress or threat, to torture or to any other form of cruel, inhuman or degrading treatment or punishment;"[168] At the initial stages of an investigation or prosecution, in fact, the Rome Statute may provide broader protection than does the U.S. Constitution the Miranda Rule requires oral notice of rights only when a defendant is interrogated in police custody;[169] the ICC statute requires such a warning whenever the prosecution has grounds to believe that the person being questioned has committed a crime. The defendant also has a right not to testify before the ICC or to refuse to make incriminating statements.[170] A defendant's invocation of the right to remain silent may not be used by the judges in determining the guilt or innocence of the defendant.[171] This safeguard appears to be analogous to the Fifth Amendment to the Constitution.

Witnesses may refuse to give testimony that might incriminate them. The ICC has the authority to give assurances to the witness that he or she will not be prosecuted or detained by the ICC for conduct prior to departure from the requested state or for incriminating testimony.[172] The ICC may also allow in camera testimony by the witness, giving assurances that the content of the testimony will not be disclosed to the public or any state.[173] Unless the ICC grants such assurances, the witness may not be compelled to answer.[174] Presumably, the right to avoid self-incrimination would extend beyond the crimes triable by the ICC to evidence which could credibly lead to prosecution by a state. It is not clear whether the ICC would respect the immunity of witnesses or accused persons granted by states, or whether it would exclude compelled testimony taken by officials of a state.

THE RIGHT TO CONFRONT WITNESSES

The Rome Statute provides that "the accused shall be entitled . . . to examine, or to have examined . . . the witnesses against him or her . . . [and]

---

[167] Rome Statute art. 54.
[168] *Id.* art. 55.
[169] *See* Wedgwood, *supra* note 141, at 123.
[170] Rome Statute art. 67(1)(g).
[171] *Id.*
[172] *Id.* art. 93(2); Draft RPE 74.
[173] Draft RPE 74.
[174] *Id.*

to obtain the attendance and examination of witnesses on his or her behalf..."[175] There is an exception, however, in cases where the alleged crime involves sexual violence or violence against children.[176] The ICC may invoke procedures to protect the identities of victims if such protection is deemed necessary.[177] Such procedures include live testimony by means of audio-visual broadcast "provided that such technology permits the witness to be examined by the Prosecutor, the defense, and by the Chamber itself, at the time that the witness so testifies," and "is conducive to the giving of truthful and open testimony and to the safety, physical and psychological well-being, dignity and privacy of the witness.[178]

U.S. law prohibits (with exceptions) the use of out-of-court statements to prove the truth of the matter stated, otherwise known as "hearsay" evidence.[179] The Rome Statute and Draft RPE do not explicitly provide for a similar rule. If the practice of the International Criminal Tribunal for the Former Yugoslavia (ICFY) is followed, hearsay evidence will likely be admissible on a more frequent basis than in U.S. courts. In civil law courts, hearsay evidence is not considered to be unduly prejudicial in most cases because the judges, unlike lay jurors, are presumed to be capable of accurately assessing the credibility of hearsay evidence and discounting any prejudicial content.

The United States Supreme Court has recognized the need for special measures for the protection of witnesses in some criminal trials, notwithstanding the defendant's right to face his accusers.[180] Measures such as one-way closed circuit television system may be employed to protect a child witness who might suffer emotional trauma at the sight of the accused, as long as sufficient safeguards were in place to preserve rigorous adversarial testing of the testimony.[181] Similar to the procedure approved by the Supreme Court, the Rome Statute provisions for protective measures must be ordered by the ICC taking into consideration all the relevant

---

[175] Rome Statute art. 67(1)(e).
[176] *Id.* art. 68.
[177] Measures to protect national security could also conflict with the accused's right to confront witnesses. *See infra* section addressing the right to a public trial.
[178] Draft RPE 67.
[179] *See* Fed. R. Evid. chapter. VIII.
[180] *See* Maryland v. Craig, 497 U.S. 836 (1990).
[181] See id.

circumstances,[182] and such measures "shall not be prejudicial to or inconsistent with the rights of the accused and a fair and impartial trial."[183]

THE PROTECTION AGAINST DOUBLE JEOPARDY

The Statute bars the ICC from trying any person who has been tried and convicted or acquitted by another court, unless that trial was for the purpose of "shielding the person concerned from criminal responsibility" or was otherwise "inconsistent with an intent to bring the person concerned to justice."[184] The *ne bis in idem* rule in the Rome Statute is in some ways more protective of the accused than the United States Constitution, which allows a person to be tried by more than one sovereign (federal or state court) or in some cases, for a separate crime arising out of the same conduct.[185] In contrast, the Rome Statute specifies the ICC may not try a person who has been tried by any other court for the same conduct, unless it finds the : trial or investigation to be improper for one of the enumerated reasons. Thus, the danger of the ICC trying a person who has already been tried by a national court will ultimately depend on the ICC's deference to national judicial decisions.[186]

The Rome Statute further provides that "no person shall be tried by another court for a crime" for which the ICC has already convicted or acquitted the person.[187] Non-parties would not be bound by this rule, however, so a person tried by the ICC could conceivably be tried again by the court of a non-party state, or possibly even by a party to the Statute that seeks to punish the same conduct under another criminal charge.

Another issue that raises possible double jeopardy implications is the prosecutorial appeal of an acquittal.[188] Under U.S. law, prosecutors may appeal only on questions of law, but may not appeal a final acquittal.[189] The

---

[182] *See id.* at 855 (distinguishing Coy v. Iowa, 487 U.S. 1012 (1988), in which similar measures were invalidated because they were imposed statutorily without requiring a case- specific inquiry into the need for protective measures).
[183] Rome Statute art. 68.
[184] Rome Statute art. 20 *(He his in idem).* "No person who has been tried by another court . . . shall be tried by the Court with respect to the sake conduct unless the proceedings in the other court [were not properly conducted]."
[185] *See* United States v. Lanza, 260 U.S. 377 (1922).
[186] *See* Christensen, *supra* note 148, at 420.
[187] *Id.* art. 20(2).
[188] See Mark C. Fleming, Appellate Review in the International Criminal Tribunals, 37TEX. INT'LL.J. 111, 117(2002).
[189] United States v. Martin Linen Supply Co., 430 U.S. 564 (1977).

Rome Statute allows the Prosecutor to appeal any decision based on procedural error, error of fact, or error of law. The defendant may also appeal on these grounds, as well as "any other ground that affects the fairness or reliability of the proceedings."[190]

THE FREEDOM FROM UNREASONABLE SEARCHES AND SEIZURES

Although the Rome Statute does not contain an express reference to the right to be free from unreasonable searches and seizures, it does provide for an exclusionary rule to prevent evidence tainted by a violation of "internationally recognized human rights."[191] The ICC will not apply national law to determine the admissibility of evidence unless it is consistent with the Rome Statute as well as treaties, principles, and rules of international law.[192] Consequently, accused persons are protected from unreasonable searches and seizures to the extent that international law forbids them. The right to privacy against such intrusion is protected under a number of international documents and treaties, including the Universal Declaration of Human Rights (UDHR)[193] and the International Covenant on Civil and Political Rights (ICCPR),[194] both of which have been ratified by a majority of nations participating at the Rome Conference.[195]

Such a standard may turn out to be higher than that applied by U.S. courts in certain cases, inasmuch as U.S. courts apply a lower standard in the event that evidence was gathered outside the territorial jurisdiction of the United States.[196] However, the ICC need not necessarily consider, for

---

[190] Rome Statute art. 81(1).
[191] See id. art. 69(7):
Evidence obtained by means of a violation of this Statute or internationally recognized human rights shall not be admissible if:
(a) The violation casts substantial doubt on the reliability of the evidence; or
(b) The admission of the evidence would be antithetical to and would seriously damage the integrity of the proceedings.
See generally George E. Edwards, International Human Rights Law Challenges to the New International Criminal Court: The Search and Seizure Right to Privacy 26 YALE J.INT'LL. 323 (2001).
[192] Rome Statute art. 21; Draft RPE 63(5).
[193] G.A. Res. 217A (III), art. 12, U.N. Doc. *N810* (1948).
[194] International Covenant on Civil and Political Rights, Dec. 16, 1966, art. 17,999 U.N.T.S. 171,6 I.L.M. 368 (entered into force Mar. 23,1976).
[195] See Edwards, *supra* note 191, at 330.
[196] For example, evidence resulting from overseas searches of American property by foreign officials may be admissible unless foreign police conduct shocks judicial conscience or

example, whether a search warrant should have been necessary. Because evidence is likely to be collected either by or with the cooperation of national law enforcement authorities, investigators will probably find it necessary to rely on national laws rather than try to discern international norms to guide the conduct of the investigation. It may therefore emerge from the ICC's practice that national laws carry more weight than the Rome Statute would suggest. At any rate, any comparison between the ICC and U.S. courts' practice with regard to tainted evidence must await the ICC's development of relevant practice. In particular, the extent to which the exclusionary rule of the ICC will apply to evidence *derived* from unlawfully seized evidence remains to be seen.

THE RIGHT TO BE PRESENT AT TRIAL

The Rome Statute provides that "[t]he accused shall be present during the trial."[197] The Trial Chamber may order the accused removed from the courtroom in exceptional circumstances when the accused causes continuous disruption, but only for such duration as is necessary, and may make provision for the accused to observe the trial and direct counsel from outside the courtroom through applicable communications technology.[198]

In U.S. jurisprudence, the Confrontation Clause of Amendment VI guarantees the accused's right to be present in the courtroom at every stage of his trial.[199] However, as long as the defendant is present at the beginning of the trial, the trial will not be rendered invalid if the defendant voluntarily absents himself during later stages of the trial.[200] The Rome Statute does not address the voluntary absence of the accused once the trial begins.

THE RIGHT TO EFFECTIVE ASSISTANCE OF COUNSEL

Article 67 of the Rome Statute provides that "the accused shall be entitled . . . to have legal assistance assigned by the Court where the interests

---

participation by V.S. agents is so substantial as to render the action that of the United States. *See* United States v. Barona, 56 P.3d 1087 (9th Cir. 1995).
[197] Rome Statute arts. 63, 67(1)(d).
[198] Rome Statute art. 63(2).
[199] Illinois v. Allen, 397 U.S. 337 (1970).
[200] Diaz v. United States, 223 V.S. 442, 455 (1912).

of justice so require, and without payment if the accused lacks sufficient means to pay for it."[201]

Defense counsel must also be well-qualified[202] according to criteria to be established.[203] The Registrar has a duty to provide adequate administrative support to the defense.[204] The Statute also guarantees that "the accused shall be entitled . . . to communicate freely with counsel of accused's choosing."[205] Similar to the attorney-client privilege practiced in the U.S. judicial system.[206] Draft RPE 73 provides that such communications are privileged and need not be disclosed at trial.

THE RIGHT TO A SPEEDY AND PUBLIC TRIAL

The U.S. Constitution guarantees the right to a speedy and public trial.[207] Similarly, the Rome Statute provides that the accused is entitled to be tried "without undue delay" by means of a public hearing.[208]

Speedy Trial

In U.S. federal courts, criminal trials generally must commence within seventy days after an indictment or original appearance before the court.[209] In courts-martial, the time limit is 120 days from the preferral of charges or the imposition of restraint, whichever date is earliest.[210] Statutes of limitations for crimes also guard against undue delay between the government's discovery of evidence and its prosecution of an accused person. A denial of the right to a speedy trial results in a dismissal of the

---

[201] Rome Statute art. 67(1)(d).
[202] Rule 22 provides: counsel for the defence shall have established competence in international or criminal law and procedure, as well as the necessary relevant experience, whether as judge, prosecutor, advocate or in other similar capacity, in criminal proceedings. A counsel for the defence shall have an excellent knowledge of and be fluent in at least one of the working languages of the Court. Counsel for the defence may be assisted by other persons, including professors of law, with relevant expertise.
[203] Rule 21.
[204] Rule 20 provides that the Registrar "shall organize the staff of the Registry in a manner that promotes the rights of the defence, consistent with the principle of fair trial as defined in the Statute."
[205] Rome Statute art. 67(1)(b).
[206] Fed. R. Evid. 501.
[207] U.S. CONST. Amend. VI.
[208] Rome Statute art. 67(1).
[209] 18 U.S.C. § 3161.
[210] Rules for Courts-Martial (R.C.M.) §707.

indictment.²¹¹ However, if the accused is found to have waived the right, or the circumstances and justice otherwise require it, a delay may not be fatal to the prosecution.²¹² In determining whether the right has been denied, a court may consider such factors as the length of the delay, the reason for the delay, whether the defendant asserted his right to a speedy trial, and the prejudice to the defendant caused by the delay.²¹³

The Rome Statute does not define "undue delay." The Draft RPE instruct the Trial Chamber to impose "strict time limits" for orders relating to discovery.²¹⁴ Draft RPE 101 provides:

In making any order setting time limits regarding the conduct of any proceedings, the Court shall have regard to the need to facilitate fair and expeditious proceedings, bearing in mind in particular the rights of the defense and the victims.

The Rome Statute does not provide a statute of limitation for any of the crimes under its jurisdiction.²¹⁵ Under U.S. law, there is no statute of limitation for the crime of genocide²¹⁶ or for any crime for which the death penalty may be imposed,²¹⁷ which includes any war crime that causes the death of its victim,²¹⁸ or any terrorism-related offense that involves the risk of death or serious injury.²¹⁹ For non-capital crimes, however, the statute of limitation is generally five years.²²⁰

Public Trial

In U.S. courts, closure of the courtroom during trial proceedings is justified only if 1) the proponent of closure advances an overriding interest likely to be prejudiced; 2) the closure is no broader than necessary; 3) the trial court considers reasonable alternatives to closure; and 4) the trial court makes findings adequate to support closure.²²¹ The right to a public trial in courts-martial is also guaranteed, but not absolute.²²² A defendant may

---

[211] Strunk v. United States, 412 U.S. 434 (1973).
[212] *See* Barker v. Wingo, 407 U.S. 514, 532 (1972).
[213] *See id.;* United States v. Baker, 63 P.3d 1478, 1497 (9th Cir. 1995).
[214] Draft RPE 84.
[215] Rome Statute art. 29.
[216] 18 U.S.C. §1091(e).
[217] 18 U.S.C. §3281.
[218] 18 U.S.C. §2441.
[219] 18 U.S.C. §3286(b).
[220] 18 U.S.C. §3282.
[221] *See* Waller v. Georgia, 467 U.S. 39, 48 (1984).
[222] R.C.M. §806.

request a closed trial, but must meet the same stringent standards applied to a request by the prosecution. Additionally, the press and public have a First Amendment right to have access to trials,[223] which must sometimes be considered in addition to the other factors.

The Rome Statute provides for public hearing unless "special circumstances require that certain proceedings be in closed session for the purposes set forth in article 68 [to protect witnesses or victims], or to protect confidential or sensitive information to be given in evidence."[224] The Trial Chamber must first give all parties notice and the opportunity to respond to any proposed special protective procedures.[225] Possible protective measures include the use of a pseudonym or technological disguise measures for witnesses, gag orders for certain information as well as its removal from the public record, or the closure of part of the hearing.[226] Additionally, any state may make an application to the ICC for necessary measures to protect its agents or sensitive national security information.[227]

RIGHT TO APPEAL

Either the defendant or the prosecutor can appeal a decision of the Trial Chamber to the Appeals Chamber based on "procedural error, error of fact or law, or disproportion between the crime and the sentence." The accused or his heirs may bring an appeal at any time based on new evidence or information that the conviction is based on false evidence, or that any of the judges or prosecutors committed any misdeeds.[228]

The ICC's opponents criticize the appeal process as inadequate because it does not provide for review outside the ICC.[229] As discussed above, the conferees sought to implement checks and balances as well as create a separation between the Appeals Division and the other trial divisions. It might also be noted that prior to 1993, international criminal courts did not include an appellate body,[230] nor did national courts review the decisions of

---

[223] *See* Richmond Newspapers v. Virginia, 448 U.S. 555 (1980).
[224] Rome Statute art. 67(7). 22SDraft RPE 87.
[225] *Id.*
[226] *Id.*
[227] Rome Statute art. 68(6).
[228] Rome Statute art. 87.
[229] *See* Casey, *supra* note 62, at 87 (arguing that the Appeals Division will have identical institutional interests t6 those of the trial chambers and would not be capable of providing truly independent review).
[230] *See* Fleming, *supra* note 188, at 112.

such tribunals.²³¹ Practice in the International Criminal Tribunal for Yugoslavia (ICTY) and the International Criminal Tribunal for Rwanda (ICTR) suggests that an appellate body within an international court may not always necessarily affirm the decisions of trial chambers.²³²

FREEDOM FROM INDEFINITE OR ARBITRARY DETENTION

The Fourth Amendment to the U.S. Constitution protects persons from unreasonable seizures, including the arrest of a person without probable cause,²³³ and sometimes, without a warrant. A person unlawfully arrested is not automatically released from custody,²³⁴ however, although evidence derived through the unlawful arrest may be excludable from evidence.²³⁵ The Fifth Amendment protects individuals from deprivation of liberty without due process of law. The Rome Statute contains corresponding safeguards to prevent the arbitrary arrest and detention of persons,²³⁶ and includes provisions for interim release of the accused prior to trial.²³⁷ Because the ICC has no law enforcement arm, relying instead largely on states to provide for the arrest and detention of accused persons using national police resources, however, the procedures may vary depending on the state of custody.

The Prosecutor must seek an arrest warrant or a summons from the Pre-Trial Chamber when necessary to ensure an accused's appearance at trial.²³⁸ The application must identify the person and the crime of which the person is accused, including a concise statement of facts supporting the allegation and a summary of evidence. On the basis of, the warrant, the ICC may request the provisional arrest or arrest and surrender under part 9 of the Rome Statute. The ICC is required to establish procedures for ensuring it is notified once a person is detained by a custodial state on the request of the ICC, and

---

[231] *See, e.g.,* Hirota v. MacArthur, 338 U.S. 197 (1948) (declining to review decision of internationally composed military commission).
[232] *See generally* Fleming, *supra* note 188.
[233] *See Ex parte* Burford, 7 U.S. (3 Cr.) 448 (1806).
[234] *See* Ker v. Illinois, 119 U.S. 436 (1886).
[235] *See* Wong Sun v. United States, 371 U.S. 471 (1963).
[236] Rome Statute arts. 55(lb), 55(ld).
[237] *Id.* arts. 59(3), 60(2).
[238] *Id.* art. 58.

must provide a copy of the warrant to the accused in a language he or she understands.[239]

The Pre-Trial Chamber is to receive notification whenever a detainee has requested interim release in accordance with the laws of the custodial state, and makes recommendations to the national court as to the suitability of release.[240] The custodial state is not permitted to consider whether the warrant was properly issued under the Rome Statute,[241] but the accused may challenge the warrant before the Pre-Trial Chamber.[242] If the accused is in the custody of the ICC, the accused may apply for interim release pending trial, which the Pre-Trial Chanlber may grant with or without conditions.[243] If the person is detained for an unreasonable period prior to trial due to inexcusable delay by the Prosecutor, the ICC may release the person, with or without conditions.[244] A person wrongfully arrested, detained, or convicted may be awarded compensation by the ICC.[245]

Once a person is convicted, the ICC will select from states willing to serve as "state of enforcement" to incarcerate the convicted person subject to any ICC conditions. The prisoner may not be tried, punished, or extradited to a third state for conduct engaged in prior to the person's incarceration without the approval of the ICC.[246] In designating a state of enforcement, the ICC must consider:

> (a) The principle that states parties should share the responsibility for enforcing sentences of imprisonment, in accordance with principles

---

[239] Draft RPE 117.
[240] *Id.* art. 59.
[241] *Id.* art. 59(4).
[242] Draft RPE 117.
[243] Draft RPE 119. Such conditions may include:
   (a) The person must not travel beyond territorial limits set by the Pre-Trial Chamber without the explicit agreement of the Chamber;
   (b) The person must not go to certain places or associate with certain persons as specified by the Pre-Trial Chamber;
   (c) The person must not contact directly or indirectly victims or witnesses; (d) The person must not engage in certain professional activities;
   (d) The person must reside at a particular address as specified by the Pre-Trial Chamber;
   (e) The person must respond when summoned by an authority or qualified person designated by the Pre-Trial Chamber;
   (f) The person must post bond or provide real or personal security or surety, for which the amount and the schedule and mode of payment shall be determined by the Pre-Trial Chamber; (h) The person must supply the Registrar with all identity documents, particularly his or her passport.
[244] Rome Statute art. 60.
[245] *Id.* art. 85; Draft RPE 173-75.
[246] Rome Statute art. 108.

of equitable distribution, as provided in the Rules of Procedure and Evidence;
(b) The application of widely accepted international treaty standards governing the treatment of prisoners;
(c) The views of the sentenced person;
(d) The nationality of the sentenced person; and
(e) Such other factors regarding the circumstances of the crime or the person sentenced, or the effective enforcement of the sentence, as may be appropriate in designating the state of enforcement.[247]

Additionally, the ICC will monitor the treatment of the prisoner, and the prisoner may petition to be moved to another state of enforcement at any time.[248]

---

[247] *Id. art. 103.*
[248] *Id.* arts. 104 and 106.

Chapter 5

IMPLICATIONS FOR THE UNITED STATES AS NON-MEMBER

The U.S. initially used the proceedings of the Preparatory Commission in part as a means of trying to rectify what it saw as the faults of the Rome Statute, and it participated as an equal during the initial conferences.[249] However, the current Administration has reduced the level of the U.S. participation,[250] and in any event, the Preparatory Commission will cease to exist after the first meeting of the Assembly of States Parties; U.S. eligibility to participate on an equal basis with other states in setting some of the ground rules for the ICC will then have ended. The Assembly of States Parties will take over as the governing body to oversee the implementation and possible amendment of the Rome Statute. Review Conferences are an alternative forum for considering amendments to the Statute; an initial Review Conference will be convened seven years after the Statute enters into effect, now expected to be July 2002. Thereafter, Review Conferences may be convened from time to time by the U.N. Secretary-General upon request by a majority of the states parties.[251] As a non-party, the United States will have no vote in either body. However, it will remain eligible to participate in both the Assembly and in Review Conferences as an observer.[252]

---

[249] *See* Scheffer, *supra* note 14, at 74.
[250] *See id.* at 63.
[251] Rome Statute art. 123.
[252] *Id.* arts. 112 and 123. States which have signed the Statute or the Final Act are eligible to participate *as* observers in both bodies. The Administration's notification of intent not to ratify the Statute should have no effect on eligibility, although it may signal an intent not to participate.

OBSERVER ROLE

The role of observers ultimately will be defined by the rules of procedure adopted for the two bodies.[253] If the current finalized draft rules are adopted, observers will be entitled to participate in the deliberations of the Assembly and any subsidiary bodies that might be established. Observer states will receive notifications of all meetings and records of Assembly proceedings on the same basis as states parties. They will not, however, be permitted to suggest items for the agenda or to make motions during debate, such as points of order or motions for adjournment. Thus, the United States may be able to participate substantially in Assembly debates as well as proffer and respond to proposals, even if it does not become a party to the Statute. The United States may also use its influence at the United Nations as a way to be heard by the Assembly of States Parties.[254]

As noted, the United States will not be able to vote in these bodies if it does not ratify the Rome Statute. It could not nominate U.S. nationals to serve as judges or cast a vote in elections for judges or the Prosecutor (or for their removal). It could not vote on the ICC's budget. It could not vote on the definition of the crime of aggression or its inclusion within the jurisdiction of the ICC, when the matter is considered at first Review Conference, or on any other amendment to the Rome Statute.

The United States, as a non-party, will have no right itself to refer situations to the Prosecutor for investigation; as a Permanent Member of the Security Council, however, it could participate as part of a Security Council referral.[255] Similarly, it could still participate in Security Council requests to the Prosecutor to defer an investigation or prosecution[256] and to the Pre-Trial Chamber to review a decision of the Prosecutor not to investigate or prosecute.[257] As a non-party to the treaty, the United States could, but would not be obligated to, cooperate with the ICC in its investigation and prosecution of crimes within its jurisdiction;[258] and under the Statute, it could, but would not be obligated to, arrest a person named in a request for

---

[253] U.N. Doc., PCNICC/2001/1/ Add.4, Draft Rules of Procedure of the Assembly of States Parties Jan. 8 (2002) (hereinafter "Draft Assembly Rules").

[254] The United Nations has a standing invitation to participate as an observer. Draft Assembly Rule 35. It may also propose items *for* the agenda. Draft Assembly Rule 11.

[255] Rome Statute art. 13. Non-parties might also be able to provide information to enable the Prosecutor to initiate a self-referred investigation, but would have no *official* role in advocating prosecution.

[256] *Id.* art. 16.

[257] *Id.* art. 53.

[258] *Id.* arts. 86, 87, and 93.

provisional arrest or for arrest and surrender from the ICC.[259] The U.S. would also retain the right not to provide information or documents the disclosure of which would prejudice its national security interests[260] and to refuse to consent to the disclosure by a state party of information or documents provided to that state in confidence.[261] Finally, as a non-party, the U.S. would not be under any obligation to contribute to the budget for the ICC, except, perhaps indirectly, to the extent that the U.N. General Assembly contributes to its support.[262]

POLITICAL IMPLICATIONS

Perspectives differ on the impact of the ICC on U.S. interests, once it begins operation. Some see the ICC as a fundamental threat to the u.s. armed forces, its political leaders, and U.S. defense and foreign policy.[263] Others see it as a valuable foreign policy tool for defining and deterring crimes against humanity, a step forward in the decades-long U.S. effort to end impunity for egregious mass crimes. Debate over the ICC has brought out a tension between enhancing the international legal justice system and encroaching on what some countries perceive as their legitimate use of force. The review by the International Criminal Tribunal for the Former Yugoslavia (ICFY) of allegations that NATO bombing in Kosovo might be deemed a war crime is illustrative of this tension. Many opponents of the ICC and members of the U.S. military were outraged that the issue was even considered. They questioned the legitimacy of the tribunal's actions, and their anger was not assuaged by the Tribunal's ultimate decision that there was "no basis for opening an investigation into any of those allegations or into other incidents relating to NATO bombing."[264] While opponents of the ICC interpret this event as an indication that the ICC is likely to pursue spurious and politically motivated cases against U.S. citizens, proponents of the ICC see it as illustrating that similar unfounded allegations would be dismissed by the ICC Prosecutor.

---

[259] *Id.* arts. 59 and 89.
[260] *Id.* art. 72.
[261] *Id..* art. 73.
[262] *Id.* art. 115.
[263] See Casey, *supra* note 62, at 849-50.
[264] *See* Final Report to the Prosecutor by the Committee Established to Review the NATO Bombing Campaign Against the Federal Republic of Yugoslavia, *available at* http://www.un.org/icty/pressreal/natoO61300.html.

The United States has often been a leader in the struggle against impunity and the quest for peace, justice and human rights. The United States led the world community in calling for establishment of the ad hoc tribunals for the former Yugoslavia and Rwanda. Supporters of the ICC argue that it could be the ultimate symbol of enforcement of basic human rights norms. Such countries, which include a number of U.S. allies, might view the true test of the U.S. commitment to international and universal concepts of justice and human rights to be its willingness to be bound by the rules established for others. From this perspective, despite the Administration's asserted intent to continue U.S. leadership in supporting human rights through means other than the ICC,[265] the U.S. refusal to ratify the Rome Statute could undermine the status of, and others' regard for, the United States as a proponent of human rights.

Others, however argue that despots like Cambodia's Pol Pot or Iraq's Saddam Hussein have not weighed possible future legal ramifications before committing massive crimes.[266] In their view, establishment of the ICC might have the effect of hardening the resolve of ruthless tyrants who may feel they have nothing to gain by giving up their power to more democratic or less ruthless regimes - as General Pinochet did in Chile or Duvalier in Haiti. The critical element from this perspective is simply the treaty's entry into force, not whether the U.S. ratifies it, other than perhaps to provide support to an argument challenging the legitimacy of the ICC.

U.S. allies, such as France and Canada, which also deploy forces abroad in peacekeeping and other interventions, initially shared U.S. concerns about the ICC's ability to judge the actions of their nationals particularly with regard to use of force. During negotiations, these countries concluded that the ICC's larger value outweighed any potential risk posed to their nationals or foreign policy. While some Americans fear the ICC could be used for political purposes, many U.S. allies see the ICC as more limited. In their view, the ICC would intervene to prosecute crimes of genocide, crimes against humanity, and war crimes only when a country fails to try its own citizens for committing such acts. Some countries are adopting war crimes provisions as part of their own domestic laws with the thought that the ICC

---

[265] *See* Grossman, *supra* note 6. However, some predict that once the ICC begins to operate, future *ad hoc* tribunals are not likely to be created, which may effectively limit the means available to support such an effort.

[266] The International Criminal Court: Hearing Before the House Committee on International Relations, 106th Cong. 4 (2000) (prepared testimony of John Bolton, Senior Vice President, American Enterprise Institute).

would never be called on to intervene. For example, France amended its constitution before ratifying the Rome Statute.[267]

For the U.S. government, the situation appears to be more complicated. With several hundred thousand persons stationed abroad, often involved in undertakings that might be subject to allegations of war crimes, the United States is particularly cautious. U.S. military leaders are especially concerned that countries that do not ratify the ICC treaty could consent to the ICC's jurisdiction over foreign peacekeeping troops for crimes committed on their territory, while declining to allow the ICC to try the persons responsible for whatever atrocities brought peacekeepers there in the first place.[268] Concern about U.S. citizens being tried by the ICC stem from an underlying fear that a politicized court could be used by hostile states as a vehicle for challenging u.s. foreign policy. Given that the ICC could exercise, jurisdiction over U.S. citizens in some situations even if the U.S. does not ratify the treaty, these concerns seem likely to persist even if the U.S. remains a non-party.

---

[267] See Appendix I - the French Solution to Constitutional Issues in the International Criminal Court: Manual for the Ratification and Implementation of the Rome Statute at the Canadian government's website on the ICC (http://209.217.98.79/english/l0_guide_e /10_guide_e.htm).

[268] See Scheffer, *supra* note 14, at 73 n.94.

Chapter 6

CONGRESSIONAL ACTION

Congress has passed several riders effectively precluding the use of funds to support the ICC.[269] The fundamental issue for Congress is whether to pass legislation to actively oppose the ICC, or whether to adopt a more benign approach aimed at encouraging the ICC to develop in a manner conducive to U.S. policy aims. There are currently two bills in Congress adopting the first approach, and one taking the second tack. The House of Representative added a rider to the Bob Stump National Defense Authorization Act for Fiscal Year 2003, H.R. 4546, expressing the sense of the Congress that "none of the funds appropriated pursuant to authorizations of appropriations in this Act should be used for any assistance to, or to cooperate with or to provide any support for, the International Criminal Court."[270] Additionally, the Administration may ask Congress to pass legislation to close jurisdictional gaps in U.S. criminal law in order to ensure U.S. territory does not become a safe haven for those accused of genocide, war crimes, and crimes against humanity.[271]

---

[269] *See* Department of Defense Appropriations for 2002, P.L. 107-117. § 8173. None of the funds made available in division A of this Act may be used to provide support or other assistance to the International Criminal Court or to any criminal investigation or other prosecutorial activity of the International Criminal Court. *See also* Departments of Commerce, Justice, and State, the Judiciary, and Related Agencies Appropriations Act, 2002 § 630, P.L.107-77.
[270] H.R. 4546 § 1034.
[271] *See* Grossman, *supra* note 6.

AMERICAN SERVICE MEMBERS' PROTECTION ACT OF 2001

The American Service Members' Protection Act (ASPA) was originally introduced in the 106th Congress as S. 2726. The proposed legislation is intended to shield members of the United States Armed Forces and other covered persons from the jurisdiction of the ICC. The Senate Committee on Foreign Relations held hearings[272] the same day the bill was introduced but did not report it. The ASPA was reintroduced in the 107th Congress as S. 857 on May 9, 2001. An amended version was introduced as S. 1610 on November 1, 2001.

Two versions of the ASPA have been passed by the House of Representatives. The first is contained in the Foreign Relations Authorization Act, Fiscal Years 2002 and 2003, H.R.1646, Title VI, subtitle B. The Senate amended version of H.R. 1646 does not include the ASPA. H.R. 1646 is in conference at the time of this writing. The second version was passed as Title II of the supplemental appropriations bill for the fiscal year ending September 30, 2002, H.R. 4775.

The Senate also passed a version of the ASPA, as part of the Departments of Commerce, Justice, and State, the Judiciary, and Related Agencies Appropriations Act, 2002, HR 3338, but it was replaced in the enacted law with language prohibiting spending to support the ICC.[273] Title II of H.R. 4775 is substantially similar to S. 857 (H.R. 1794), and would repeal the provision passed as part of H.R. 3338. Title VI, subtitle B of H.R. 1646 is summarized below, followed by a description of the additional language contained in Title II of H.R. 4775.

The ASPA would prohibit cooperation with the ICC on the part of any agency or entity of the federal government, or any state or local government. (Sec. 634) Covered entities are prohibited from responding to a request for cooperation by the ICC or providing specific assistance, including arrest, extradition, seizure of property, asset forfeiture, service of warrants, searches, taking of evidence, and similar matters. It prohibits agents of the ICC from conducting any investigative activity on U.S. soil related to matters of the ICC. Sec. 634(d) states that the United States "shall exercise its rights to limit the use of assistance provided under all treaties and

---

[272] *The International Criminal Court: Protecting American Servicemen and Officials from the Threat of International Prosecution, Hearing before the Senate Comm. on Foreign Relations,* 106th Cong. (2000).

[273] P.L.107-117 § 8173. *See supra* note 269.

executive agreements for mutual legal assistance in criminal matters . . . to prevent . . . use by the [ICC of such assistance]." It does not ban the communication to the ICC of U.S. policy or assistance to defendants. Sec. 636 requires the President to put "appropriate procedures" in place to prevent the direct or indirect transfer of certain classified national security information to the ICC.

The ASPA would further restrict U.S. participation in U.N. peacekeeping operations to missions where the President certifies U.S. troops may participate without risk of prosecution by the ICC because the Security Council permanently exempted U.S. personnel for prosecution for activity conducted as participants, or because each other country participating in the mission is either not a party to the ICC and does not consent to its jurisdiction, or has entered into an agreement "in accordance with article 98" of the Rome Statute.[274] It also prohibits military assistance to any non-NATO country that is member of the ICC, unless the President waives the restriction (Sec. 637).

Sec. 638 authorizes the President to use "all means necessary and appropriate" to bring about the release of covered United States and allied persons,[275] upon the request of the detainee's government, who are being detained or imprisoned by or on behalf of the ICC. The Act does not provide a definition of "necessary and appropriate means" to bring about the release of covered persons, other than to exclude bribes and the provision of other such incentives. The language could arguably be interpreted to authorize the use of armed force to conduct rescue operations to free some prisoners charged with war crimes, genocide, or crimes against humanity.

The President may waive the restrictions on participation in peacekeeping operations and providing military assistance for a renewable period of one year after notifying appropriate congressional committees of his intent to do so and reporting that the ICC has entered into a binding agreement that prohibits it from exercising jurisdiction over covered u.s. and allied persons (from certain countries for so long as those countries have not

---

[274] Rome Statute art. 98 prohibits the ICC from pursuing requests for assistance or surrender that would require the requested state to act inconsistently with its international obligations.
[275] "Covered allied persons" includes military personnel, elected or appointed officials, and other persons working for a NATO country or a major non-NATO ally, which includes Australia, Egypt, Israel, Japan, Jordan, Argentina, the Republic of Korea, and New Zealand, or Taiwan, "so long as that government is not a party to the International Criminal Court and wishes its officials and other persons working on its behalf to be exempted from the jurisdiction of the [ICC]." Sec. 642(3). Coveted allies currently could include persons from the Czech Republic, Turkey, Australia, Egypt, Israel, Japan, the Republic of Korea, and Taiwan. (Of these countries, only Turkey, Taiwan, and Japan have not signed the Rome Statute.) 276H;R. 4775 § 2011; *see also* S. 1610 § 11.

ratified the treaty). (Sec. 633) The President may also waive some requirements with respect to a specific "named individual," if there is reason to believe the named individual is guilty of the charge, it is in the national interest of the United States for the ICC to prosecute the person, and that during the investigation, no covered U.S. or allied person will be arrested, detained, prosecuted, or imprisoned by or on behalf of the ICC with regard actions taken in their official capacities.

H.R. 4775. The version of the ASPA included in H.R. 4775 (which is substantially similar to the Senate amended version of HR 3338) contains an additional exception at section 2011, stating that the restrictions on cooperation with the ICC (sec. 2004 of H.R. 4775) and protecting classified information (sec. 2006) do not apply to "any action or actions with respect to a specific matter taken or directed by the President on a case-by-case basis in the exercise of the President's authority as Commander in Chief of the Armed Forces of the United States under article II, section 2 of the United States Constitution or in the exercise of the executive power under article II, section 1 of the United States Constitution."276 The section would require the President to notify Congress within 15 days of the action, unless such notification would jeopardize national security. It further clarifies that "nothing in [the] section shall be construed as a grant of statutory authority to the President to take any action." Sec. 2012 prohibits delegation of the authorities vested in the President by secs. 2003 (waiver provision) and 2011(a) (constitutional exception).

Inasmuch as sections 2004 and 2006 are already subject to presidential waiver under section 2003(c) in the case of the investigation or prosecution of a "named individual," it appears that this section is drafted to avoid possible conflicts of the separation of powers between the President and Congress. In the event that the President takes the position that the prohibitions of sections 2004 and 2006 infringe upon his constitutional authority in certain cases, he might assert that Congress has no power even to require a waiver under section 2003. Section 2011 appears to ensure notification of Congress, at least at some point after the action has been taken, regardless of whether the President believes that sections 2004 and 2006 impinge his constitutional authority.

The effect of sec. 2011 is not entirely clear, depending as it does on the interpretation of the President's executive powers under article II, section 1 of the Constitution and his authority as Commander in Chief of the Armed Forces. Interpreted broadly, the constitutional executive power includes the power to execute the law, meaning the execution of *any* law, whether statutory or constitutional, or even international law. Such an interpretation would seem to render the waiver provision of sec. 2003(c) superfluous. Interpreted narrowly, the executive authorities cited above could refer to those powers which the President does not share with Congress. Under a narrow interpretation, Congress would be deemed to be without authority to regulate such actions in any event, in which case it would appear to make little sense to restrict its application to sections 2004 and 2006. The language could be construed by a court to imply a waiver authority apart from the restrictions outlined in section 2003.

THE AMERICAN SERVICE MEMBER AND CITIZEN PROTECTION ACT OF 2002

The American Service Member and Citizen Protection Act of 2002, H.R. 4169, introduced April 11, 2002, issues findings that under the U.S. Constitution and international law, the President's signature on a treaty without ratification by the Senate is not binding on the United States, and that therefore the ICC Statute has no validity with respect to U.S. The bill proclaims the Rome Statute to be "ultra vires" (sec. 2(9)) and in violation of international law, the American Declaration of Independence, and the Constitution (sec. 2(12)). It also urges the President to rescind the U.S. signature and take steps (sec. 3) to prevent the establishment of the ICC. Sec. 4 prohibits the expenditure of funds for use in any manner for the "establishment or operation of the [ICC]" (with a penalty of 5 years or $50,000 for violations, sec. 6). Sec. 5 provides that actions against U.S; soldiers shall be considered to be an act of aggression, and actions against other U.S. persons shall be considered "to be an offense against the law of nations."

THE AMERICAN CITIZENS' PROTECTION AND WAR CRIMINAL PROSECUTION ACT OF 2001

This bill, S.1296 (H.R. 2699), seeks a more conciliatory approach to the ICC, providing that the President should certify that the ICC "has established a demonstrated record of fair and impartial prosecution of genocide, war crimes, and crimes against humanity" before the Rome Statute is submitted to the Senate for its advice and consent. (Sec. 10). Sec. 4 provides a sense of the Congress that the United States should "maintain a policy of fully supporting the due process rights of all United States citizens before foreign tribunals, including the [ICC]". It recommends the U.S. government participate as an observer in the Assembly of States Parties in order to ". . .a protect and further U.S. interests. Sec. 8 requires the President to ensure appropriate procedures are in place to protect national security information.

Sec. 5 prohibits the United States from taking any action to extradite U.S. citizens and service members to the ICC if the accused is investigated or prosecuted in a U.S. court, and urges the United States to exercise its right to assert jurisdiction over such persons (to invoke complementarity), unless the President determines it is not in the national interest. If a U.S. citizen is prosecuted by the ICC, the President "shall use appropriate diplomatic and legal resources to ensure that such person receives due process . . ." and provide whatever exculpatory evidence may be available to assist the accused. Sec. 7 authorizes support to the ICC on a case-by-case basis if such support would serve important U.S. interests, particularly if the victims of the crimes alleged are citizens of the United States or friendly countries.

The bill contains a number of reporting requirements for assessments of the operation of the ICC and its effects on U.S. interests. Sec. 6 outlines reporting procedures, requiring the President to compare due process protections afforded to persons before the ICC to those afforded U.S. service members under status of forces agreements, and to bilateral or multilateral extradition treaties. Sec. 5 requires the Administration to conduct a study to determine what statutory amendments may be necessary to close jurisdictional gaps in the criminal code or Uniform Code of Military Justice. Sec. 9 requires a report on command arrangements that could place U.S. service members at risk of prosecution by the ICC and measures taken to mitigate the risks.

INDEX

A

accused persons, 28, 40, 43, 48
accused, 2, 5, 6, 11, 13, 14, 28, 31, 33-35, 37, 39-42, 44-46, 48, 49, 62
act of aggression, 26, 31, 61
ad hoc tribunals, 5, 54
alleged crime, 7, 32, 41
alleged perpetrators, 27, 36
American citizen(s), 32, 38
American Citizens' Protection and War Criminal Prosecution Act of 2001, 61
American Service Member and Citizen Protection Act of 2002, 61
American Service Members' Protection Act (ASPA), 58, 59, 60
appeals chamber, 11, 12, 29, 47
appeals division, 11, 12, 47
armed conflicts, 24, 35
Assembly of States Parties, 1, 8-10, 12, 14, 15, 18, 37, 51, 52, 62
atrocities, 4, 27, 35, 55

B

Bob Stump National Defense Authorization Act, 57
Bush Administration, vii, 1, 3, 31

C

children, 14, 19, 23, 24, 41
China, 3
Clinton, President, 3
coercion, 40
compensation, 12, 49
conflict of interest, 11
Confrontation Clause of Amendment VI, 44
Constitution, 35, 37, 38, 40, 45, 48, 60, 61
constitutional exception, 60
constitutional standards, 37
conviction, 11, 39, 47
court martial, 25, 38
courtroom, 44, 46
courts, national, 4, 28, 35, 47
courts-martial, 25, 39, 45, 46
crime of aggression, 1, 8, 25, 52
crimes against humanity, 1, 4, 5, 17, 19-21, 53, 54, 57, 59, 61
criminal law, 9, 14, 18, 21, 45, 57
criminal responsibility, 13, 42
cruel, inhuman or degrading treatment or punishment, 40
custodial state, 48, 49

D

death penalty, 46
Declaration of Independence, 61
deputy prosecutor, 12
dispute the charges, 12
domestic courts, 32, 33
double jeopardy, 42
drug trade, 33
due process rights, 33, 62
duress, 40

E

East Timor, 2
enforcing sentences, 49
ethnic minorities, 5
exonerating evidence, 13

F

fair and impartial trial, 42
Fifth Amendment, 40, 48
First Amendment, 47
foreign policy, 53-55
former Yugoslavia, 54
Fourth Amendment, 48

G

gag orders, 47
Geneva Conventions, 22-25, 27, 35
Geneva Protocols, 25
genocidal policies, 5
genocide, 1, 17-19, 34, 35, 54, 57, 59, 61
Germany, 14
guilt, 39, 40

H

Hague Conventions, 21
hearsay, 41
hostile countries, 6

human rights, vii, 1, 15, 43, 54
Hussein, Saddam, 54

I

imprisonment, 21, 49
incriminating information, 13
incriminating statements, 40
innocence, 39, 40
interim release, 48, 49
internal armed conflicts, 5
international community, vii, 1, 17, 26
international court, vii, 1, 3, 4, 5, 48
International Covenant on Civil and Political Rights (ICCPR), 43
International Criminal Court (ICC), vii, 1-7, 9-11, 13-15, 17-20, 22, 25-37, 39-43, 47-55, 57-62
international criminal court, 2, 26, 31
International Criminal Tribunal for Rwanda (ICTR), 4, 48
International Criminal Tribunal for the Former Yugoslavia (ICFY), 38, 41, 53
International Criminal Tribunal for Yugoslavia (ICTY), 4, 48
international crises, 6
international documents, 43
international law, 3, 9, 20-25, 27, 33, 43, 60, 61
international legal justice system, 53
international legal personality, 9
investigations, 11, 12, 13
Iran, 3
Iraq, 3, 54
Israel, 3, 59

J

Japan, 59
judicial decisions, national, 42

jurisdiction, vii, 1-7, 11, 12, 17, 18, 20-22, 25, 27-35, 38, 39, 43, 46, 52, 55, 58, 59, 62

K

Kosovo, 53

L

law enforcement, 44, 48
legal assistance, 44, 59
legal systems, 10, 18
Libya, 3
limited jurisdiction, 4
local government, 58

M

member states, 10, 12, 18
military insignia, 22
military personnel, 6, 21, 32, 39, 59
misconduct, 10, 12
model of jurisdiction, 5

N

national police, 48
national security, 11, 41, 47, 53, 59, 60, 62
nationality, 4, 5, 20, 27, 28, 31-33, 50
NATO, 25, 26, 53, 59
Nazi, 4
negotiations, vii, 4, 28, 38, 54
non-capital crimes, 46
non-governmental organizations (NGOs), 30
non-judicial administration, 13
non-ratifying country, vii, 4
Nuremberg, 4, 6, 19, 26

O

Office of the Prosecutor, 9, 11, 12

opposing forces, 5
out-of-court statements, 41
overzealous prosecutors, 9

P

peacekeeping mission(s), 2, 6, 22, 24
pending trial, 49
Permanent Five, 7, 28
perpetrator(s), 4, 5, 19, 20, 24, 27, 29, 35
Pinochet, General, 54
police custody, 40
political decision making, 13
political leaders, 53
political support, 5
post-World War II tribunals, 4
Pot, Pol, 54
prejudice, 46, 53
prejudicial, 11, 39, 41, 42
Preparatory Commission, 4, 7, 9, 14, 19, 26, 34, 37, 51
Preparatory Committee, 4, 18
presidency, 9, 10, 14
pre-trial chamber, 9, 12, 29-31, 34, 39, 48, 49, 52
pre-trial division, 11
principles of equitable distribution, 50
prison uniform, 39
privacy, 11, 41, 43
probable cause, 48
procedural rules, vii, 4
procedural safeguards, vii, 4, 37, 38
prosecution, 2, 5, 7, 12, 25, 26, 27, 29, 33-35, 40, 45, 47, 52, 59-62
prosecutor, 6, 12, 13, 14, 28-32, 34, 39, 41, 43, 48, 49, 52, 53
prosecutorial appeal, 42
protective measures, 41, 42, 47
public hearing, 45, 47
public record, 47
public trial, 41, 45, 46

R

rape, 23, 24
reasonable basis, 12, 30, 34
registry, 9, 13, 14, 45
relevant evidence, 11
relief supplies, 23
review conference, 51, 52
right to confront witnesses, 40
right to remain silent, 40
risk of death, 46
Rome Conference, 3, 4, 7, 18, 25, 27, 43
Rome Statute, vii, 1-7, 9, 10, 12-15, 17, 18, 20-22, 25-35, 37, 38, 40-49, 51, 52, 54, 55, 59, 61
Rome Treaty, 2, 3, 13, 38
Rule of Procedure and Evidence (RPE), 14, 29-31, 37, 39-41, 43, 45-47, 49
Rules of Procedure, 4, 30, 37, 50, 52
Rwanda, 19, 54

S

safeguards, 41, 48
secret ballot, 12, 13
Security Council, 5, 7, 26, 28, 31, 32, 34, 52, 59
security of witnesses, 11
self-incrimination, 40
serious injury, 20, 22, 46
speedy trial, 45
starvation of civilians, 23
state of enforcement, 49, 50
Sudan, 3
Supreme Court, 38, 41
survivors, 12

T

territorial jurisdiction, 20, 21, 29
territorial limits, 49
territorial state, 32
terrorism-related offense, 46
threat, 26, 31, 40, 53
torture, 21, 23, 40
treaties, 18, 25, 27, 43, 58, 62
trial by jury, 38
trial chamber(s), 11, 12, 29, 30, 39, 44, 46-49
trial division(s), 9, 10, 11, 12
trial proceedings, 46
trumped-up allegations, 27

U

U.N. Charter, 26, 28, 31
U.N. General Assembly, 4, 26, 53
U.N. Security Council, 4-7, 12, 14, 26, 28, 30, 31
U.S. defense, 53
U.S. soldiers, vii, 3
Uniform Code of Military Justice (UCMJ), 25, 38, 62
United Nations, vii, 1, 3, 4, 9, 22, 24, 26, 52
United States Constitution, 42, 60
Universal Declaration of Human Rights (UDHR), 43
unlawful arrest, 48
unreasonable searches and seizures, 43
uses of force, vii, 3

V

veto, 5, 7, 26, 28, 32
Victims and Witnesses Unit (VWU), 13
victims, 4, 13, 19, 20, 41, 46, 47, 49, 62
violation of international law, 61

W

war crime(s), vii, 1-3, 6, 17, 20-22, 25, 31, 35, 46, 53-55, 57, 59, 61

war crimes provisions, 54
war criminals, 4, 5, 27
warrant, 34, 44, 48, 49

witnesses, 13, 40, 41, 47, 49
world community, 54